1st International Workshop on Artificial Intelligence for Historical Image Enrichment and Access (AI4HI-2020)

Marseille, France
11 – 16 May 2020

Editors:

Yalemisew Abgaz
Amelie Dorn
Jose Luis Preza Diaz
Gerda Koch

ISBN: 978-1-7138-1253-1

Printed from e-media with permission by:

Curran Associates, Inc.
57 Morehouse Lane
Red Hook, NY 12571

Some format issues inherent in the e-media version may also appear in this print version.

Association for Computational Linguistics
209 N. Eighth Street
Stroudsburg, Pennsylvania 18360

Phone: 1-570-476-8006
Fax: 1-570-476-0860

acl@aclweb.org

Additional copies of this publication are available from:

Curran Associates, Inc.
57 Morehouse Lane
Red Hook, NY 12571 USA
Phone: 845-758-0400
Fax: 845-758-2633
Email: curran@proceedings.com
Web: www.proceedings.com

LREC 2020 Workshop
Language Resource and Evaluation Conference
11–16 May 2020

1st International Workshop on Artificial Intelligence for Historical Image Enrichment and Access (AI4HI-2020)

PROCEEDINGS

Editors:
Yalemisew Abgaz, Adapt Centre, Dublin City University
Amelie Dorn, Austrian Academy of Sciences, Vienna, Austria
Jose Luis Preza Diaz, Austrian Academy of Sciences, Vienna, Austria
Gerda Koch, AIT Forschungsgesellschaft mbH, Europeana Local AT

Proceedings of the LREC 2020 First International workshop on Artificial Intelligence for Historical Image Enrichment and Access (AI4HI-2019)

Edited by:
Yalemisew Abgaz, Amelie Dorn, Jose Luis Preza Diaz, and Gerda Koch

Acknowledgements:
The workshop is supported by the ChIA Project funded by the go!digital programme of the Austrian Academy of Sciences and the ADAPT Centre at Dublin City University.

For more information:
European Language Resources Association (ELRA)
9 rue des Cordelières
75013, Paris
France
http://www.elra.info
Email: lrec@elda.org

Preface

AI4HI-2020 is a major forum that brings together participants from various disciplines to present, discuss, disseminate and share insights on the exploitation of Artificial Intelligence (AI) techniques, semantic web technologies and language resources for the semantic enrichment, search and retrieval of cultural images for the first time. The workshop is co-located with the 12th Edition of Language Resources and Evaluation Conference at the Palais du Pharo, Marseille, France.

Semantic web technologies are capable of enriching the data with the required semantics; however, existing ontologies and available models do not fully support the domain-specific requirements of users. The workshop attracts significant attention to make historical images accessible to the general public, as more domain-specific semantics becomes available. The AI4HI-2020 workshop has a general focus on the application of artificial intelligence, semantic web technologies such as ontologies, thesauri and controlled vocabularies, and language resources to enrich and improve access to images related (but not limited) to historical and cultural heritage. This workshop provides the platform to discuss research results including experiments, use cases, experiences, best practices, methods and recommendations for the use of AI and semantic web technologies for historical images. The workshop attracted papers from many stakeholders including AI researchers, NLP experts, digital humanists, linguists, computer scientists and ontology engineers together to present their work and share their experiences.

Y. Abgaz, A. Dorn, J. L. Preza Diaz, G. Koch

11-16 May 2020

Organising Committee

- Yalemisew Abgaz, Adapt Centre, Dublin City University
- Amelie Dorn, Austrian Academy of Sciences, Vienna, Austria
- Jose Luis Preza Diaz, Austrian Academy of Sciences, Vienna, Austria
- Gerda Koch, AIT Forschungsgesellschaft mbH, Europeana Local AT

Program Committee

- Renato Rocha Souza, Austrian Academy of Sciences, Vienna, Austria
- Anna Fensel, Semantic Technology Institute (STI), University of Innsbruck, Austria
- John Roberto, Adapt Centre, Dublin City University, Dublin, Ireland
- Nicole High-Steskal, Department for Image Science, Danube University Krems
- Chao-Hong Liu, Dublin City University, Dublin, Ireland

Table of Contents

Workshop Program

14:30–16:00 **Session 1**

14:30–14:40 ***Welcoming Speech***

14:40–15:10 *Enriching Historic Photography with Structured Data using Image Region Segmentation*
Taylor Arnold and Lauren Tilton

15:10–15:30 *Interlinking Iconclass Data with Concepts of Art & Architecture Thesaurus*
Anna Breit

14:30–16:00 **Session 2**

14:30–15:00 *Toward the Automatic Retrieval and Annotation of Outsider Art images: A Preliminary Statement*
John Roberto, Diego Ortego and Brian Davis

15:00–15:15 *Automatic Matching of Paintings and Descriptions in Art-Historic Archives using Multimodal Analysis*
Christian Bartz, Nitisha Jain and Ralf Krestel

15:15–15:30 *Towards a Comprehensive Assessment of the Quality and Richness of the Europeana Metadata of food-related Images*
Yalemisew Abgaz, Amelie Dorn, Jose Luis Preza Diaz and Gerda Koch

15:30–15:50 **Concluding Remarks and Next Step**

Proceedings of the 1st International Workshop on Artificial Intelligence for Historical Image Enrichment and Access (AI4HI-2020), pages 1–10
Language Resources and Evaluation Conference (LREC 2020), Marseille, 11–16 May 2020

Enriching Historic Photography with Structured Data using Image Region Segmentation

Taylor Arnold[†], **Lauren Tilton**[*]
[†]Department of Mathematics and Computer Science, University of Richmond
[*]Department of Rhetoric and Communication Studies, University of Richmond
410 Westhampton Way, Richmond, VA, USA 23173
{tarnold2, ltilton}@richmond.edu

Abstract

Cultural institutions such as galleries, libraries, archives and museums continue to make commitments to large scale digitization of collections. An ongoing challenge is how to increase discovery and access through structured data and the semantic web. In this paper we describe a method for using computer vision algorithms that automatically detect regions of "stuff"—such as the sky, water, and roads—to produce rich and accurate structured data triples for describing the content of historic photography. We apply our method to a collection of 1610 documentary photographs produced in the 1930s and 1940 by the FSA-OWI division of the U.S. federal government. Manual verification of the extracted annotations yields an accuracy rate of 97.5%, compared to 70.7% for relations extracted from object detection and 31.5% for automatically generated captions. Our method also produces a rich set of features, providing more unique labels (1170) than either the captions (1040) or object detection (178) methods. We conclude by describing directions for a linguistically-focused ontology of region categories that can better enrich historical image data. Open source code and the extracted metadata from our corpus are made available as external resources.

Keywords: computer vision, image segmentation, cultural heritage, photography, Linked Data, ontology, digital humanities

1. Introduction

Galleries, libraries, archives, and museums (known as GLAM institutions) and other cultural heritage organizations have increasingly sought to provide structured metadata about historic collections in an effort to increase access and discovery. Where records have been digitized and rights restrictions allow for it, many of these organizations have also been able to make the digital records directly accessible through openly available APIs and URIs. Prominent examples of these efforts include the Rijksmuseum's *RijksData* (Dijkshoorn et al., 2018), Europeana's Search API, Record API, and SPARQL endpoint (Concordia et al., 2009), and the *Linked Data Service* provided by the United States Library of Congress (Zimmer, 2015). The effort to make resources available within a cohesive semantic web offers exciting possibilities for research and public access to cultural collections. Yet, challenges remain for producing structured data that facilitates access and exploration of digital archives.

Many digital collections held by cultural heritage organizations consist of still and moving image data. These include scans of textual documents, photographs of material culture, and digital scans of artwork, photographs and other visual objects. Unlike machine-readable textual archives, visual collections do not immediately offer a simple method for automated search or data extraction. While records may include extensive metadata about the provenance of a digital image, there is often little to no structured data pertaining to the content of the image itself. Even when descriptive captions exist, these are typically short and intended to be read alongside the object itself. In other words, captions are written assuming that the reader will be able to look at the object. The lack of structured linguistic descriptions serves as a roadblock to providing rich links between and across collections, as well as limiting the possibilities for large-scale analysis. While expert and crowd-sourced annotations can fill in some gaps, manual data construction requires extensive resources and becomes more difficult as digitized datasets increase in size (Seitsonen, 2017).

Computer vision techniques provide a direction for the automated creation of structured data to enrich collections of historic digital images. Machine learning techniques can detect features present in images and store these alongside human-generated metadata pertaining to the digital records. However, the use of automated techniques have their own unique set of challenges. Most computer vision algorithms are built using modern datasets, and may produce annotations that are inaccurate or inappropriate for historic data. Incorrectly extracted data records are particularly concerning when making data available to the public. Even when including confidence scores for extracted features, studies have shown that people have trouble accurately interpreting probabilistic data and are overly confident in predictions (Khaw et al., 2019). The challenges of mis-classified data are particularly acute when they risk reinforcing racial, gender, and socioeconomic biases inherent in the training data behind machine learning techniques. For example, a recent study showed that face detection algorithms have difficulty identifying darker skinned individuals (Buolamwini and Gebru, 2018). Applying state-of-the-art face detection algorithms to a collection of photographs, therefore, risks further hiding marginalized communities.

In this article we present a method for the automated extraction of highly-accurate structured data describing the content of historic photography using computer vision algorithms. Specifically, our approach is based on the detection of regions of the image containing elements described as

Figure 1: Automatically generated labels assigned to FSA-OWI color photographs by the Mask R-CNN instance object classification algorithm (X101-FPN) (Wu et al., 2019). For each of the eight selected object types, the five images from the FSA-OWI color photographs that are most predicted to contain the given category are shown. All categories were estimated to exist with probability greater than 80%. The plane and horse categories seem to have correctly identified the objects in their five respective images, and two of the cow images are in fact cows (the others are horses). The remaining categories seem to be all false detections. Many mistakes are hard to explain, such as the row of skateboard objects.

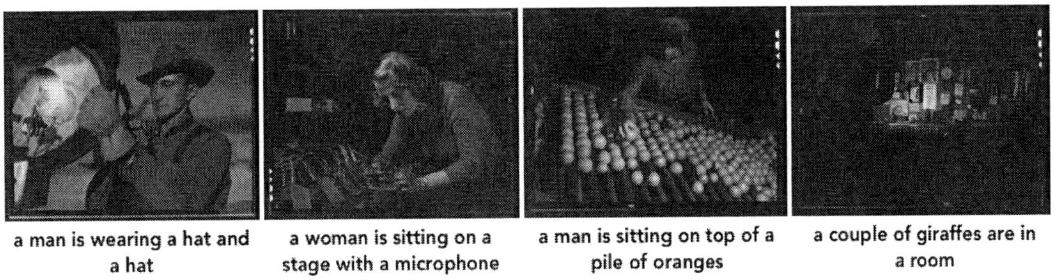

Figure 2: Three detected captions for three FSA-OWI photographs using the 'Show, attend and tell' model (Xu et al., 2015). The first provides a caption that matches the image and the third produces a caption that is very similar to the image. The second correctly identifies the subject of a woman in the frame but mistakenly believes she is holding a microphone. The final image produces an annotation that incorrectly labels the people as giraffes.

"stuff", which includes elements such as sky, water, trees, grass, and roads (Caesar et al., 2018). While temporal, cultural, and regional differences exist in some of these categories, the stuff-based regions of images are significantly more robust than many other features that can currently be extracted from image data.

We focus on the application of our method to the 1610 color photographs from the Farm Security Administration-Office of War Information Collection (FSA-OWI) at the United States Library of Congress. We selected the collection for three reasons. First, it is a part of one of the most famous and researched photography archives from the United States (Tagg, 2009). Second, the collection is held by a library that is invested in open access and encourages experimentation with their digital collections. Third, the collection is indicative of many documentary photography collections held in GLAM institutions. It is a large enough collection that manual annotation of new features would be overly time consuming and expensive. It has has some descriptive metadata consisting of minimal captions, but these are too short and vauge to easily facilitate semantic connections within and across collections.

The remainder of this article is structured as follows. Section 2 gives a brief survey of several projects currently using computer vision and structured data to augment historic image collections. Section 3 provides an overview of image segmentation and the current approaches for the classification of stuff categories. Section 4 presents our specific approach and schema for producing structured data from images. In Section 5 we give an evaluation of our approach applied to a collection of 1610 photographs from the 1930s and 1940s. We conclude in Section 6 with a discussion of future possibilities and challenges of applying image segmentation to historic datasets.

2. Background

The task of enriching image datasets with automated descriptions has been approached from several angles. Methods include object detection (2.1), automated captions (2.2) and image embeddings (2.3). The objects of study in historic datasets often do not align with the contemporary categories used to describe object detection algorithms, automated captions, and the types of relationships produced by image embeddings. Working with historic data to produce the kinds of automated extraction of structured data necessary requires a different approach, which we outline in the sections that follow.

2.1. Object Detection

The algorithmic identification of objects within an image is one of the most prominent tasks in computer vision. Early tasks focused on relatively simple objectives, such as the classification of hand-written digits in the MNIST dataset, which used small 28-by-28 grids of black and white pixels (Platt, 1999). Modern training datasets feature thousands of categories, ranging for very specific categories, such as a specific species of dogs, to relatively abstract concepts such as 'grocery stores' and 'parties'. Using transfer learning, in which a model trained on one dataset is modified to function on a new task, it is possible to produce algorithms trained to detect virtually any object category by manually tagging only a small set of training examples. The training of models for specific features has been employed in the annotation of several historical image datasets, such as the location of Dadaism art work (Thompson and Mimno, 2017) and detecting figures in digitized newspapers (Wevers and Smits, 2019).

Current state-of-the-art models for detecting objects within images are difficult to use as a general-purpose code system for the analysis of visual culture. Available models feature categories that are too specific and only cover a very small number of the object types that could be seen within the frame of modern, western-centric film and photography. When considering historical or more diverse datasets, the coverage is even worse. For example, the popular ILSVRC dataset contains 1000 categories, but only seven types of fruits (fig, pineapple, banana, pomegranate, apple, strawberry, orange, and lemon), four vegetables (cucumber, artichoke, bell pepper, head cabbage), and eight other food items (pretzel, bagel, pizza, hotdog, hamburger, guacamole, burrito, and popsicle) (Russakovsky et al., 2015). There are no generic catch-all food categories for other items falling outside of these lists. While there are 120 subcategories

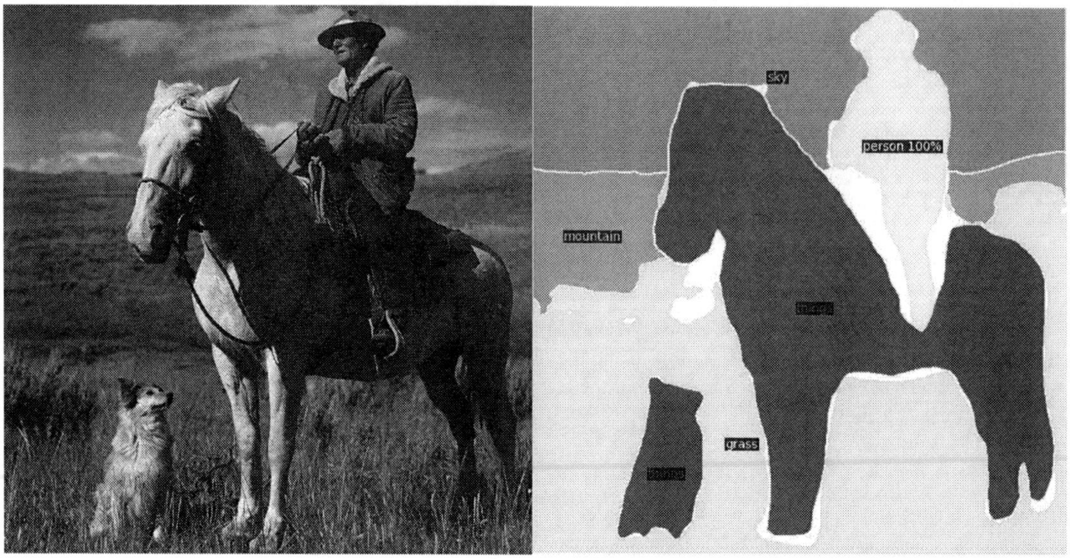

Figure 3: Example of a trained stuff-segementation algorithm applied to one FSA-OWI photograph (Wu et al., 2019). The algorithm detected five types of regions: sky, mountain, grass, things, and person.

for dog breeds, there is no category pertaining to horses or cows. Applying these object detection models indiscriminately to a large corpus without understanding its limitations will result in biased results. They will find certain kinds of food items, animals, and clothing, but will completely ignore examples outside of a narrowly curated list of categories.

Object detection is a useful tool for annotating specific features of interest within a collection. However, each feature requires a manually trained model and may not generalize well to a new collection. Using existing models with preselected categories on historic images typically produces a mix of correct and false annotations. Figure 1 shows the results of a popular object detection algorithm to the FSA-OWI collection (Wu et al., 2019). While some categories produced reasonably accurate annotations, such as the detection of horses and people, most categories detected more false positives than successfully generated tags. Without a good general-purpose collection of object detectors, a challenge discussed further in Section 6 , object detection remains difficult to use as a means for producing structured data for linking historic image collections.

2.2. Automated Captions

Because object detection on its own has major challenges, particularly when working with historic data, another method has been to use automated captions. The automated generation of descriptive image captions is a more ambitious task that has been a popular line of research at the intersection of computational linguistics and computer vision. Captions generated through neural networks with the help of linked textual data have shown to be fairly accurate, offering a useful tool for automated description of images in news articles and other media powerful (Hessel et al., 2019) (Batra et al., 2018) (Hollink et al., 2016). As with object detection, automatically generated captions within well-defined domains, such as profile photos, has also been fairly successful at generating accurate descriptions (Gatt et al., 2018). On the more general task of generating free-form image captions, current state-of-the-art methods also produce impressive results when applied to modern datasets (Nikolaus et al., 2019) (Jiang et al., 2019) (Wang et al., 2018). On datasets that differ from the specific training data, however, modern methods too-often produce nonsensical results that make them difficult to deploy directly in an archive. Figure 2 show the results of one popular caption algorithm applied to photographs from the 1940s (Xu et al., 2015). While two captions produce reasonable results, a third incorrectly identifies the object held by the main subject and the fourth mistakenly believes the two men in the frame are giraffes.

2.3. Image Embedding

Given the difficulty of automatically producing accurate structure data from image collections, the use of image embedding has become a popular approach for finding links between and across collections of visual data. Similar to the process of using word embeddings, image embeddings most frequently project a collection of images into the penultimate layer of a neural network. Once represented as a sequence of numbers in a high-dimensional space, images within an across collections can be associated with their closest neighbors (McAuley et al., 2015). Flattening image embeddings into two or three dimensions produces useful visualizations of large image collections. Tools in the digital humanities, such as Yale DH Lab's *PixPlot*, make this approach accessible to a large community of users and illustrates the appeal of its method (Duhaime, 2019).

Group	Meta Categories	Categories
indoor	ceiling	ceiling-tile
indoor	floor	floor-wood; floor-stone; floor-tile; floor-marble; carpet
indoor	food	fruit; vegetable; salad
indoor	furniture	cabinet; cupboard; counter; desk; door; light; mirror; shelf; stairs; table
indoor	rawmaterial	cardboard; metal; paper; plastic
indoor	textile	banner; blanket; curtain; cloth; clothes; napkin; mat; pillow; rug; towel
indoor	wall	wall-brick; wall-stone; wall-tile; wall-wood; wall-panel; wall-concrete
indoor	window	window-blind
outdoor	building	bridge; house; roof; skyscraper; tent
outdoor	ground	dirt; gravel; pavement; platform; playingfield; railroad; road; sand; snow; mud
outdoor	plant	flower; grass; tree; bush; leaves; branch; moss; straw
outdoor	sky	clouds
outdoor	solid	mountain; rock; hill; stone; wood
outdoor	structural	fence; net; railing; cage
outdoor	water	river; sea; waterdrops; fog

Table 1: Hierarchical description of 91 stuff categories (Caesar et al., 2018). Additionally, each metacategory other than "rawmaterial" also contains an "other" label (not shown) for regions that do not fit into any specific category.

For finding similar images or detecting patterns and trends within a collection, image embeddings are a useful tool and generalize well to new and historic datasets. By forgoing the explicit creation of structured data, they avoid many of the pitfalls of the automated information extraction. However, the constructed data does not produce meaningful relationships that can be easily distributed as structured data. This makes it difficult to extend the recommendation system to new collections and to find links across a web of archives.

3. Image Segementation of Stuff

A recent development in computer vision has opened an exciting new path for the automated description of images. In 2018, a research team from University of Edinburgh and Google AI released a new corpus of image training data that contained 91 new categories (Caesar et al., 2018). However, unlike previous image datasets, their categories did not focus on the detection of specific objects. Rather, the team built an ontology and large collection of training data to detect the "amorphous background regions" within an image. These regions do not correspond to objects, but instead to un-enumerable collections such as the sky, water, and ceilings. The team described these regions as "stuff" categories and proposed a comprehensive ontology of them. Their approach split all regions under two groups: "indoor stuff" and "outdoor stuff". These groups are further divided into meta categories, which include "water", "ground", "sky", "furniture", and "floor". Finally, these are split into 91 fine-grained categories such as "sea", "mud", "clouds", and "carpet". A full description of the available categories is given in Table 1. The joint task of identifying these labels alongside object labels has been one of shared tasks sponsored by the Common Objects in Context challenge from 2017 to 2019 (Kirillov et al., 2019). As a result, there are now many accurate models for automatically labelling these regions. Figure 3 shows the detected regions found within an image from the FSA-OWI archive.

While no classification scheme can be free of cultural assumptions nor account for all possible scenarios, the stuff categories are significantly more generic than the object categories. This is particularly true of the high- and mid-level categories. The higher-level categories avoid some of the material-specific designations from the lowest-level categories, such as wood flooring, that may not be applicable with images that significantly depart from the available training data. By aggregating information about detected stuff categories, we can make intelligent guesses about whether an image was taken inside or outside, how the people in the image are placed relative to the background, and the location and role of the horizon in framing the image.

As always when working with automatically generated annotations, care should be taken to avoid misinterpreting the results of stuff-segmentation algorithms. There are categories that have a degree pf ambiguity between them, such as "dirt" and "sand" or "mat" and "rug". Also, the stuff categories were designed pragmatically for the task of assigning all the pixels in an image to a fixed set of classifications. The distinction between stuff and objects is not a sharp epistemological distinction. Several categories overlap between the two, such as "furniture" and "door"; the difference in labels is a result of the size of the images and their resolution rather than a fundamental property of the objects themselves. These ambiguities are essentially unavoidable and should not deter the usage of the stuff categories. The only caution is to avoid making claims that may come down to relatively arbitrary distinctions between categories—for example, claiming that Photographer A took more photos with dirt backgrounds whereas Photographer B preferred sand backgrounds—without carefully evaluation the appropriateness of the distinction and the accuracy of the automatic identification in a particular application.

4. Annotations as Structured Data

Our proposed method for the automatic extraction of structured data from image data begins by applying the Detectron2 implementation of image stuff segmentation (Wu et

```
@prefix rdf:       <http://www.w3.org/1999/02/22-rdf-syntax-ns#> .
@prefix pgram:     <http://photogrammar.org#> .
@prefix dcterms:   <http://purl.org/dc/terms/> .
@prefix oa:        <http://www.w3.org/ns/oa#> .

<http://photogrammar.org/anno1> a oa:Annotation ;
  dcterms:creator <http://photogrammar.org/tarnold2> ;
  dcterms:created "2020-02-19T12:00:00Z" ;
  oa:hasBody [
    a                    pgram:ImageSegmentationRegion ;
    pgram:regionName     <http://example.org/stuff/things> ;
    pgram:regionPercent  32 ;
  ] ;
  oa:hasTarget <http://photogrammar.org/resource/1a35022v> ;
  oa:motivatedBy oa:tagging .

<http://photogrammar.org/anno2> a oa:Annotation ;
  dcterms:creator <http://photogrammar.org/tarnold2> ;
  dcterms:created "2020-02-19T12:01:00Z" ;
  oa:hasBody [
    a                    pgram:ImageSegmentationRegion ;
    pgram:regionName     <http://example.org/stuff/people> ;
    pgram:regionPercent  6 ;
    pgram:regionCount    1 ;
  ] ;
  oa:hasTarget <http://photogrammar.org/resource/1a35022v> ;
  oa:motivatedBy oa:tagging .
```

Schema 1: Example of extracted structured data from the image in Figure 3 using the stuff-based image segmentation technique.

al., 2019). The total proportion of the image allocated to each stuff category is computed from the annotated image. For any category that constitutes more than 5% of the total image, we store an annotation relating the category to the image, along with the overall percentage score. Additionally, we tabulate the number of detected people in the image. While the general purpose object detections are not reliable on historic images, the detection of the people category is reasonably accurate across different corpora and the presence (or absence) of people within an image is an important feature to distinguish different image subjects.

The utility of structured data rests on describing data using standard ontologies. It is important, when extracting data for linkage and discovery, to carefully consider the schema(s) to use in describing relationships. There currently exist several ontologies for describing image data. Schema.org supplies generic schemas for photographs, images, paintings, and creative works (Guha et al., 2016). Dublin core offers a well-established ontology for describing digital records specifically designed for libraries and digital archives (Weibel, 1997). Both of these are useful for describing the provenance of digital objects. Several schema also exist for describing the content of image data, often with a specific focus on describing time-coded moving images such as film and television. The *Advene* project provides an ontology designed to integrate with their manually annotation tool (Aubert and Prié, 2005). The *Audio-Visual Rhetorics of Affect* group extended this vocabulary to include more granular terms that capture formal elements of affect and film studies (Agt-Rickauer et al., 2018).

The field-specific ontologies provided for digital images provide useful methods for linking collections. Our digital project based on the FSA-OWI collection uses the Dublin Core Metadata Element Set to describe each record. In our work here, however, we aim for simplicity by describing our annotations using a class extension of the the Web Annotation Data Model (Sanderson et al., 2017). Schema 1 shows any example of the extracted structured data from regions detected in the image from Figure 3. Each detected region type within an image is assigned a unique identifier describing the region. This region is then associated with the original image, the type of region and the percentage of area taken up by the region. For the person annotation, the number of individual objects (1) is also recorded. Not shown in the example is a structured description of the region type codes that encode the hierarchical relationships described in Table 1. The title of the image is included to indicate where other image-level metadata would be recorded—such as the photographer, date, and rights information—in the full record.

5. Evaluation

The annotation method described in Section 4 was applied to the entire corpus of 1610 color photographs from the FSA-OWI collection (Trachtenberg, 1990). An example of these are shown in Figure 4. For the purpose of comparison, two additional annotations were also computed. Each photograph was tagged with detected objects and labelled with any object that appeared with at least a probability of 85%

Figure 4: Seven selected stuff types and the people category shown with the five images from the FSA-OWI color photographs that are most predicted to contain the given type. Uses the ResNet+FPN model provided by the Detectron2 model zoo (Wu et al., 2019). The only labels that appears the be falsely detected are in the third and fifth bridge images, where construction equipment is falsely believed to be a bridge.

and for each photograph an automatically detected caption was produced (Figures 1-2 show examples of these annotations).[1] The annotations for each photograph were coded to indicate where the annotation was accurately applied. A "stuff" region label was considered accurate if the region was visible within the image and an object label was considered accurate if the object existed somewhere in the image. A caption was considered accurate if it could be considered true in a strictly literal sense. For example, a caption saying that there are two people in an image that contains three people was considered correct for our purpose. Because not all images are guaranteed to include a region that falls above our threshold for inclusion, we also recorded the percentage of images that had at least one corresponding label (called recall in the results). The results are given in Table 2.

	Acc.	Recall	Unique Results
Stuff & People	97.5%	98.9%	1140
Objects	70.7%	37.3%	178
Captions	31.5%	100%	1040

Table 2: Results of manually validated labels produced on the FSA-OWI color photographs.

Both the close-analysis of the annotations in Figure 4 illustrate the efficacy of "stuff" region-based annotations for adding structured data to historic image data. The object annotations do offer many useful features, but have an error rate around 30%, making them difficult to use without manual validation. At the moment the captions are correct less than a third of the time, and even the best captions fall far short of human-produced records. The "stuff" regions have an accuracy of 97.5%; while public display of estimated annotations should contain a note about their auto-generated nature, it is possible to use these annotations without manual validation. The high accuracy of the stuff-based annotation method does not come at the cost of producing only uninteresting or unexpressive relations. In fact, the number of uniquely labelled images is slightly higher than even the captions-based method, and labels were found for nearly 99% of all images. Looking manually at the results of the most representative images, we see that the stuff-categories capture key features of most of the image backgrounds and many of their foregrounds.

6. Conclusions and Future Directions

We have presented a method for the automated production of structured data describing the content of photographic-corpora. The robustness and efficacy of our method was shown through a case-study using 1610 documentary photographs from the 1930s and 1940s. While other methods, such as object-detection and automated caption generation, have the potential to provide additional structured data, the generalizability of our approach offers a strategy for algorithmically enriching large corpora of photographic materials through structured data in order to facilitate access, discovery, and exploration within and across collections.

The approach presented here offers several avenues for further extensions to supply additional structured information to historic image corpora. First, there are a number of ways that we could further encode information about the detected regions. For example, recording the dominant colors of each region type or indicating what part of an image a region is located. Secondly, it is possible to develop a structured language for creating image captions from the structured data. In connection with the first item, this would lead to captions such as a "Photograph of two people, with a green mountain and blue sky in the background". This could produce image captions that, while more predictable than techniques allowing for free-form language, are also significantly more accurate. Finally, and most ambitiously, would be to construct a generic, hierarchical version of a tagged object detection algorithm that simulates the stuff-based regions. This would allow for a similar usage of object-detection algorithms for the automated extraction of objects in the foreground of an image without being constrained to narrowly defined categories selected by current datasets.

[1] Full replication code, data, and results are available at: `https://github.com/statsmaths/fsa_color_analysis`.

7. Acknowledgements

Work supported by a National Endowment for the Humanities Digital Advancement Grant (HAA-261239-18) and the Andrew W. Mellon Foundation's *Collections as Data: Part to Whole* initiative.

8. Bibliographical References

Agt-Rickauer, H., Hentschel, C., and Sack, H. (2018). Semantic annotation and automated extraction of audio-visual staging patterns in large-scale empirical film studies. In *SEMANTICS Posters&Demos*.

Alexiev, V. (2018). Museum linked open data: Ontologies, datasets, projects. *Digital Presentation and Preservation of Cultural and Scientific Heritage*, (VIII):19–50.

Alikhani, M., Nag Chowdhury, S., de Melo, G., and Stone, M. (2019). CITE: A corpus of image-text discourse relations. In *Proceedings of the 2019 Conference of the North American Chapter of the Association for Computational Linguistics: Human Language Technologies, Volume 1 (Long and Short Papers)*, pages 570–575, Minneapolis, Minnesota, June. Association for Computational Linguistics.

Aubert, O. and Prié, Y. (2005). Advene: active reading through hypervideo. In *Proceedings of the sixteenth ACM conference on Hypertext and hypermedia*, pages 235–244.

Baldwin, S. (1968). Poverty and politics; the rise and decline of the farm security administration.

Batra, V., He, Y., and Vogiatzis, G. (2018). Neural Caption Generation for News Images. In Nicoletta Calzolari (Conference chair), et al., editors, *Proceedings of the Eleventh International Conference on Language Resources and Evaluation (LREC 2018)*, Miyazaki, Japan,

May 7-12, 2018. European Language Resources Association (ELRA).

Buolamwini, J. and Gebru, T. (2018). Gender shades: Intersectional accuracy disparities in commercial gender classification. In *Conference on fairness, accountability and transparency*, pages 77–91.

Caesar, H., Uijlings, J., and Ferrari, V. (2018). COCO-stuff: Thing and stuff classes in context. In *Proceedings of the IEEE Conference on Computer Vision and Pattern Recognition*, pages 1209–1218.

Chen, H., Zhang, H., Chen, P.-Y., Yi, J., and Hsieh, C.-J. (2018). Attacking visual language grounding with adversarial examples: A case study on neural image captioning. In *Proceedings of the 56th Annual Meeting of the Association for Computational Linguistics (Volume 1: Long Papers)*, pages 2587–2597, Melbourne, Australia, July. Association for Computational Linguistics.

Concordia, C., Gradmann, S., and Siebinga, S. (2009). Not (just) a repository, nor (just) a digital library, nor (just) a portal: A portrait of europeana as an api. In *World Library and Information Congress: 75th IFLA General Conference and Council*.

Dijkshoorn, C., Jongma, L., Aroyo, L., Van Ossenbruggen, J., Schreiber, G., Ter Weele, W., and Wielemaker, J. (2018). The rijksmuseum collection as linked data. *Semantic Web*, 9(2):221–230.

Duhaime, D. (2019). PixPlot: Visualize large image collections with WebGL. `https://github.com/YaleDHLab/pix-plot`.

Fan, Z., Wei, Z., Wang, S., and Huang, X. (2019). Bridging by word: Image grounded vocabulary construction for visual captioning. In *Proceedings of the 57th Annual Meeting of the Association for Computational Linguistics*, pages 6514–6524, Florence, Italy, July. Association for Computational Linguistics.

Gatt, A., Tanti, M., Muscat, A., Paggio, P., Farrugia, R. A., Borg, C., Camilleri, K., Rosner, M., and der Plas, L. V. (2018). Face2Text: Collecting an Annotated Image Description Corpus for the Generation of Rich Face Descriptions. In Nicoletta Calzolari (Conference chair), et al., editors, *Proceedings of the Eleventh International Conference on Language Resources and Evaluation (LREC 2018)*, Miyazaki, Japan, May 7-12, 2018. European Language Resources Association (ELRA).

Gella, S. and Keller, F. (2018). An evaluation of image-based verb prediction models against human eye-tracking data. In *Proceedings of the 2018 Conference of the North American Chapter of the Association for Computational Linguistics: Human Language Technologies, Volume 2 (Short Papers)*, pages 758–763, New Orleans, Louisiana, June. Association for Computational Linguistics.

Guha, R. V., Brickley, D., and Macbeth, S. (2016). Schema. org: evolution of structured data on the web. *Communications of the ACM*, 59(2):44–51.

Hartmann, M. and Søgaard, A. (2018). Limitations of cross-lingual learning from image search. In *Proceedings of The Third Workshop on Representation Learning for NLP*, pages 159–163, Melbourne, Australia, July. Association for Computational Linguistics.

Hessel, J., Savva, N., and Wilber, M. (2015). Image representations and new domains in neural image captioning. In *Proceedings of the Fourth Workshop on Vision and Language*, pages 29–39, Lisbon, Portugal, September. Association for Computational Linguistics.

Hessel, J., Lee, L., and Mimno, D. (2019). Unsupervised discovery of multimodal links in multi-image, multi-sentence documents. In *Proceedings of the 2019 Conference on Empirical Methods in Natural Language Processing and the 9th International Joint Conference on Natural Language Processing (EMNLP-IJCNLP)*, pages 2034–2045, Hong Kong, China, November. Association for Computational Linguistics.

Hollink, L., Bedjeti, A., van Harmelen, M., and Elliott, D. (2016). A corpus of images and text in online news. In Nicoletta Calzolari (Conference Chair), et al., editors, *Proceedings of the Tenth International Conference on Language Resources and Evaluation (LREC 2016)*, Paris, France, may. European Language Resources Association (ELRA).

Jiang, M., Hu, J., Huang, Q., Zhang, L., Diesner, J., and Gao, J. (2019). REO-relevance, extraness, omission: A fine-grained evaluation for image captioning. In *Proceedings of the 2019 Conference on Empirical Methods in Natural Language Processing and the 9th International Joint Conference on Natural Language Processing (EMNLP-IJCNLP)*, pages 1475–1480, Hong Kong, China, November. Association for Computational Linguistics.

Khaw, M. W., Stevens, L., and Woodford, M. (2019). Individual differences in the perception of probability. *Available at SSRN 3446790*.

Kirillov, A., He, K., Girshick, R., Rother, C., and Dollár, P. (2019). Panoptic segmentation. In *Proceedings of the IEEE conference on computer vision and pattern recognition*, pages 9404–9413.

Kiros, J., Chan, W., and Hinton, G. (2018). Illustrative language understanding: Large-scale visual grounding with image search. In *Proceedings of the 56th Annual Meeting of the Association for Computational Linguistics (Volume 1: Long Papers)*, pages 922–933, Melbourne, Australia, July. Association for Computational Linguistics.

Lin, T.-Y., RoyChowdhury, A., and Maji, S. (2015). Bilinear CNN models for fine-grained visual recognition. In *Proceedings of the IEEE international conference on computer vision*, pages 1449–1457.

Mason, R. and Charniak, E. (2012). Apples to oranges: Evaluating image annotations from natural language processing systems. In *Proceedings of the 2012 Conference of the North American Chapter of the Association for Computational Linguistics: Human Language Technologies*, pages 172–181, Montréal, Canada, June. Association for Computational Linguistics.

McAuley, J., Targett, C., Shi, Q., and Van Den Hengel, A. (2015). Image-based recommendations on styles and substitutes. In *Proceedings of the 38th International ACM SIGIR Conference on Research and Development in Information Retrieval*, pages 43–52.

Mensink, T. and Van Gemert, J. (2014). The Rijksmuseum challenge: Museum-centered visual recognition. In *Proceedings of International Conference on Multimedia Retrieval*, pages 451–454.

Nikolaus, M., Abdou, M., Lamm, M., Aralikatte, R., and Elliott, D. (2019). Compositional generalization in image captioning. In *Proceedings of the 23rd Conference on Computational Natural Language Learning (CoNLL)*, pages 87–98, Hong Kong, China, November. Association for Computational Linguistics.

Platt, J. C. (1999). Using analytic qp and sparseness to speed training of support vector machines. In *Advances in neural information processing systems*, pages 557–563.

Russakovsky, O., Deng, J., Su, H., Krause, J., Satheesh, S., Ma, S., Huang, Z., Karpathy, A., Khosla, A., Bernstein, M., et al. (2015). ImageNet large scale visual recognition challenge. *International journal of computer vision*, 115(3):211–252.

Sadler, P., Scheffler, T., and Schlangen, D. (2019). Can neural image captioning be controlled via forced attention? In *Proceedings of the 12th International Conference on Natural Language Generation*, pages 427–431, Tokyo, Japan, October–November. Association for Computational Linguistics.

Sanderson, R., Ciccarese, P., and Young, B. (2017). Web annotation data model. `https://www.w3.org/TR/annotation-vocab/`. Accessed: 2020-02-19.

Seitsonen, O. (2017). Crowdsourcing cultural heritage: public participation and conflict legacy in finland. *Journal of Community Archaeology & Heritage*, 4(2):115–130.

Sharma, P., Ding, N., Goodman, S., and Soricut, R. (2018). Conceptual captions: A cleaned, hypernymed, image alt-text dataset for automatic image captioning. In *Proceedings of the 56th Annual Meeting of the Association for Computational Linguistics (Volume 1: Long Papers)*, pages 2556–2565, Melbourne, Australia, July. Association for Computational Linguistics.

Shimizu, N., Rong, N., and Miyazaki, T. (2018). Visual question answering dataset for bilingual image understanding: A study of cross-lingual transfer using attention maps. In *Proceedings of the 27th International Conference on Computational Linguistics*, pages 1918–1928, Santa Fe, New Mexico, USA, August. Association for Computational Linguistics.

Singhal, K., Raman, K., and ten Cate, B. (2019). Learning multilingual word embeddings using image-text data. In *Proceedings of the Second Workshop on Shortcomings in Vision and Language*, pages 68–77, Minneapolis, Minnesota, June. Association for Computational Linguistics.

Tagg, J. (2009). *The disciplinary frame: Photographic truths and the capture of meaning*. U of Minnesota Press.

Thompson, L. and Mimno, D. (2017). Computational cut-ups: The influence of dada. *The Journal of Modern Periodical Studies*, 8(2):179–195.

Trachtenberg, A. (1990). *Reading American Photographs: Images as History-Mathew Brady to Walker Evans*. Macmillan, London, England.

van Miltenburg, E., Elliott, D., and Vossen, P. (2018). Measuring the diversity of automatic image descriptions. In *Proceedings of the 27th International Conference on Computational Linguistics*, pages 1730–1741, Santa Fe, New Mexico, USA, August. Association for Computational Linguistics.

Vinyals, O., Toshev, A., Bengio, S., and Erhan, D. (2016). Show and tell: Lessons learned from the 2015 MS COCO image captioning challenge. *IEEE transactions on pattern analysis and machine intelligence*, 39(4):652–663.

Wang, J., Madhyastha, P. S., and Specia, L. (2018). Object counts! bringing explicit detections back into image captioning. In *Proceedings of the 2018 Conference of the North American Chapter of the Association for Computational Linguistics: Human Language Technologies, Volume 1 (Long Papers)*, pages 2180–2193, New Orleans, Louisiana, June. Association for Computational Linguistics.

Weibel, S. (1997). The Dublin Core: a simple content description model for electronic resources. *Bulletin of the American Society for Information Science and Technology*, 24(1):9–11.

Wevers, M. and Smits, T. (2019). The visual digital turn: Using neural networks to study historical images. *Digital Scholarship in the Humanities*.

Wu, Y., Kirillov, A., Massa, F., Lo, W.-Y., and Girshick, R. (2019). Detectron2. `https://github.com/facebookresearch/detectron2`.

Xu, K., Ba, J., Kiros, R., Cho, K., Courville, A., Salakhudinov, R., Zemel, R., and Bengio, Y. (2015). Show, attend and tell: Neural image caption generation with visual attention. In *International conference on machine learning*, pages 2048–2057.

Yokota, M. and Nakayama, H. (2018). Augmenting Image Question Answering Dataset by Exploiting Image Captions. In Nicoletta Calzolari (Conference chair), et al., editors, *Proceedings of the Eleventh International Conference on Language Resources and Evaluation (LREC 2018)*, Miyazaki, Japan, May 7-12, 2018. European Language Resources Association (ELRA).

Zhao, S., Sharma, P., Levinboim, T., and Soricut, R. (2019). Informative image captioning with external sources of information. In *Proceedings of the 57th Annual Meeting of the Association for Computational Linguistics*, pages 6485–6494, Florence, Italy, July. Association for Computational Linguistics.

Zimmer, M. (2015). The Twitter archive at the library of congress: Challenges for information practice and information policy. *First Monday*, 20(7).

Proceedings of the 1st International Workshop on Artificial Intelligence for Historical Image Enrichment and Access (AI4HI-2020), pages 11–15
Language Resources and Evaluation Conference (LREC 2020), Marseille, 11–16 May 2020

Interlinking Iconclass Data with Concepts of Art & Architecture Thesaurus

Anna Breit[1]
[1]Semantic Web Company, Austria; [1]anna.breit@semantic-web.com

Abstract

Iconclass, being a well established classification system, could benefit from interconnections with other ontologies in order to semantically enrich its content. This work presents a disambiguating and interlinking approach which is used to match Iconclass Subjects and concepts of the Art and Architecture Thesaurus. In a preliminary evaluation, the system is able to produce promising predictions, though the task is highly challenging due to conceptual and schema heterogeneity. Several algorithmic improvements for this specific interlinking task, as well as and future research directions are suggested. The produced matches, as well as the source code and additional information can be found at `https://github.com/annabreit/vocabulary-interlinking`.

Keywords: Ontology Matching, Word Sense Disambiguation, Semantic Enrichment, Iconclass, AAT

1. Introduction

Iconclass (IC) (Van De Waal et al., 1973) is a widely used resource to annotate and describe iconographic content of artworks. Its entities are highly specific, where one IC entry often represents an entire scene. However, due to its narrative and descriptive focus, it is difficult to semantically exploit these entities. An art recommender for example would benefit from a semantic enrichment of IC entities, as it could better understand the content of artworks favoured by the user and thus his preferences. The interlinkage with a more general ontology would increase the semantic interpretability, both for machines and humans.

This work aims to semantically enrich IC data by interlinking IC Subjects — a controlled vocabulary used to annotate IC concepts — with concepts of the Art and Architecture Thesaurus (AAT) (Peterson, 1990). A novel interlinking algorithm is introduced and preliminarily evaluated on a non-expert annotated dataset, yielding promising results. Still existing weaknesses of the proposed system are addressed in an extensive discussion on suggestions for improvement.

2. Data Sources

2.1. Iconclass (IC)

Iconclass is a well established taxonomy-like classification system published between 1973 and 1985 by the Royal Netherlands Academy of Arts and Sciences. It contains iconographic entities which are widely used by museums and art institutions around the world to describe the content of artwork images. The entities are mainly hierarchically organised, where the hierarchy is reflected in the identification code: Iconclass data is subdivided into 10 root nodes — so-called "main-divisions" — with corresponding ID-codes of the digits 0-9. For each level of depth added, the identification code is expanded by either (1) an alphanumeric digit, to introduce a subdivision (a child node with increased specificity), (2) bracketed text, to introduce a specific entity (like a person) as child node, or (3) bracketed text starting with a plus-sign, to "add a 'shade of meaning' to the definition or meaning"[1] via the child node.

IC entities are quite heterogeneous: While the main divisions 1 to 5 describe general topics to represent principal elements of art — such as *44D211 tax payment* — entities whose ID starts with a digit ranging from 6 to 9 are more narrative, describing specific religious or mythological scenes and elements, like *94L3221 the Hydra is killed by Hercules assisted by Iolaus, who sears the roots of the severed heads with burning brands; an enormous crab nips Hercules' foot*. The main division 0 is used for abstract art. Moreover, even entities describing general topics can be both concept-centric like *44D211 tax payment* or action-centric like *34C11 feeding wild animals in winter*.

To further describe IC entities, *Subjects* were introduced. Subjects are tag-like, elements based on a controlled case sensitive vocabulary. IC entities can have Subjects in multiple languages, however, the tags are not interlinked across languages. Moreover, a 1-to-1 matching between languages is not possible, as there is a different amount of tags per language for some Subjects. Even though Subjects are disambiguated, the specificity varies which sometimes makes it hard to understand the range of the intended meaning: The subject *plate* is for example used for *41B2133 hearth-plate*, *41D11 fashion plates*, and *48C6143 plate, film ~ photography*. Subjects are inherited which means that an IC concept is annotated both with its individual Subject tags as well as with all tags from all of its broader concepts.

2.2. Art & Architecture Thesaurus (AAT)

The Art & Architecture Thesaurus is a ontology describing art, architecture, conservation, archaeology, and other cultural heritage, covering a broad temporal and geographic spectrum. Included are not only entries for objects, but also those describing colours, materials, art-styles and -periods. This wide range of concepts is divided into 7 main facets: Associated Concepts, Physical Attributes, Styles and Periods, Activities, Agents, Materials, and Objects. Facets are further divided into one or multiple hierarchies with a systematic focus. Entries within the AAT hierarchy can have different record types, i.e. *facet*, *concept*, *hierarchy name* and *guilde term*. For most of the facets, only general concepts but no instances exist. For example, while *300417304 sun gods* is in the AAT, the Egyptian god *Ra* will not be found. However, there are exceptions to this rule where named entities are required to describe a concept, e.g. art-styles and -periods or a specific type of furniture.

3. Problem Statement

As described above, AAT and IC, though both being ontologies in the same domain, have very different foci which

[1]http://www.iconclass.nl/contents-of-iconclass

makes matching quite challenging. Not only is the entity overlap of these two resources limited, but also the hierarchical structure of the entries that do have a matching equivalent in the other ontology are fundamentally different. Matching AAT and IC data on concept level would therefore not add much information to the entities. However, Subjects used in IC can be seen as a more general description of the concept which better resembles the nature of AAT concepts.

Therefore, in this work, the two resources are not interlinked by matching their concepts, but IC Subjects are interlinked with AAT concepts to add a layer of semantics. To be more precise, the task of ontology matching of a source and a target ontology is reformulated as the alignment between a controlled vocabulary, which annotates a source ontology, and a target ontology. Due to this restatement, classical ontology matching algorithms — especially based on structure-level matchers — can not be applied intuitively, as IC Subjects are not structured.

4. Related Work

The idea of matching Iconclass Subjects and AAT concepts was first explored by Weda in 2017 (Weda, 2017). He used two different data management and alignment tools, i.e., OpenRefine[2] and Cultuurlink[3], to align the two taxonomies based on lexical features. Weda provided a comprehensive qualitative report on the matching results, allowing insight on difficulties arising with the alignment of the two ontologies. Unfortunately, the resulting matches were not made publicly available.

The first work to explicitly exploit IC Subjects in order to add semantic richness to IC concepts within a real world use case was provided by (David and Kamerling, 2019). The authors presented a recommendation system for artworks based on relevancy scores of the interconnected IC and AAT concepts.In the proposed algorithm, the concepts of the two resources were aligned via IC Subjects, meaning that the IC concept is linked to all AAT conceps, to which at least one of its IC Subjects matches. This means, that the same Subject can be matched with different AAT concepts, depending on the IC concept it was attached to. To create the matches between IC Subjects and AAT concepts, first candidate matches were created using a simple string matcher. Then disambiguation was performed using a proprietary algorithm, where a match is considered correct if at least one of the other IC Subjects assigned to the Iconclass concept could be found in the hierarchical AAT parent path, or, if only one candidate match was found. Unfortunately, this algorithm produced many false positive matches.

In order to improve the interlinking of IC and AAT data this work presents an algorithm for matching IC Subjects and AAT concepts directly. This gives the possibility to better understand the meaning of an IC Subject, by being able to analyse the IC concept it analyses. Herefore, a sophisticated disambiguation algorithm is introduced, which classifies each candidate match independently and therefore is capable of producing an arbitrary number of matches for each instance.

[2]http://openrefine.org/

[3]http://cultuurlink.beeldengeluid.nl/app

5. Matching strategy

As mentioned in 2., the specificity of the meaning of IC Subjects varies among the tags, resulting in IC Subjects aggregating the meaning of several AAT concepts. Therefore, the matching algorithm must be able to take one, multiple and no correct matches into account. Also, Word Sense Disambiguation has to be performed, as various terms appear more than once with different meanings within the resources. For example, the term "craft" exists as an English IC Subject, while AAT contains four concepts having "craft" as prefLabel or altLabel: *300212527 aircraft, 300212528 spacecraft, 300042940 watercraft* and *300054704 crafts (art genres)*. To determine which of these AAT concepts actually fit to the IC Subject *craft*, some kind of context for both the IC Subject and AAT concepts is necessary. By comparing these contexts, disambiguation can be performed and a decision on which are correct matches can be made.

5.1. The algorithm

Let $\{s_0, s_1, s_2, ...s_n\}$ be the elements of the source resource S to be matched to the target resource T. Each s_i has zero, one or multiple matching candidates $\{t_0^i, t_1^i, ..., t_m^i\} \in T$. The aim is to disambiguate the matching candidates in order to identify correct matches.

For each $s_i \in S$, three different levels of context C_i^1,C_i^2 and C_i^3 can be defined, where C_i^1 corresponds to the narrowest context which best describes s_i, while C_i^3 corresponds to the broadest one having only a distant relation to s_i. Each element $t_j^i \in T$ is associated with a context Z_j. These contexts are dependent on the resources to be matched and must be defined by the user. For deciding whether the candidate t_j^i should actually match with s_i the overlap between their contexts is calculated as follows:

$$D(s_i, t_j^i) = \frac{\sum_{k=1}^{3} \alpha_k \cdot \phi(C_i^k, Z_j)}{\sum_{k=1}^{3} \alpha_k \cdot \sigma(C_i^k)}$$

with

$$\phi(X,Y) = \begin{cases} \sqrt[\lambda]{\frac{|X \cap Y|}{|X|}}, & if|X| > 0 \\ 0, & otherwise \end{cases}$$

and

$$\sigma(X) = \begin{cases} 1, & if|X| > 0 \\ 0, & otherwise \end{cases}$$

$\alpha_k \in [0,1]$ and $\lambda \in N$ are hyperparameters. The resulting $D(s_i, t_j^i)$ corresponds to the disambiguation value. If it is higher than a certain threshold h, the tuple $(s_i$,$t_j^i)$ is considered a match.

6. Experiment

A preliminary experiment was performed on matching IC Subjects and AAT concepts in order to achieve a first insight on the suitability and remaining challenges of the proposed matching procedure. IC and AAT data was extracted in October 2019. The produced matches of all English IC Subjects, as well as the source code and additional information can be found at `https://github.com/annabreit/vocabulary-interlinking`.

6.1. Setup

For matching IC Subjects S to AAT concepts T , the following contexts were defined:

- C_i^1 **: Content in label parentheses.**
  Subject labels may contain additional content in parentheses which adds additional meaning to the label. This content helps to disambiguate the label either directly e.g. *square (shape)*, or by further describing it (*Deadly Sins (Seven)*, *left (opposite to right)*).
- C_i^2**: Direct sibling Subjects.**
  This context contains Subjects that were co-assigned to the same IC concept as the Subject of interest s_i. However, only the individual Subjects of the concept are taken into account, inherited Subjects are filtered out.
- C_i^3**: Inherited sibling Subjects**
  This context contains Subjects that were co-assigned to the same IC concept as the Subject of interest s_i. However, only inherited Subjects are taken into account.
- Z_j**: Broader concepts**
  For all "preferred broaders" of the concept of interest t_j^i, prefLabels and altLabels are added to this context.

Matching candidates were collected by performing language-aware case-insensitive exact string matching for lightly pre-processed subject labels of IC and prefLabels and altLabels from AAT concepts. Pre-processing of Subject labels consists of the removal of content in parenthesis. The hyperparameters were experimentally set to, $\alpha_1 = 0.9$, $\alpha_2 = 0.8$ and $\alpha_3 = 0.7$, while λ was set to 5. The threshold parameter h was chosen to be 0.2. The decision of using such a low threshold is based on the known different structure of the two ontologies. The overlap between the contexts will be small, especially for Subjects that are also used in IC concept describing narrative content. For example, *94L3221 the Hydra is killed by Hercules assisted by Iolaus, who sears the roots of the severed heads with burning brands; an enormous crab nips Hercules' foot* has 16 inherited Subjects and 5 individual ones, including *crab*. Here, *crab* will collect a lot of context Subjects which will most likely not help to disambiguate, such as *foot*, *history* or *twelve*. Therefore, already a small amount of matching elements in the different contexts can be seen as a strong indicator of an actual match.

6.2. Evaluation Set

To estimate the matching quality and to get an impression of remaining problems, an evaluation set was created and manually evaluated by two non-experts. As the focus lays on the disambiguation capability of the matching algorithm, the evaluation set consists of 100 randomly selected English IC Subjects from those that had multiple matching candidates. Candidate matches were created for these 100 Subjects, resulting in 242 total potential matches to be evaluated.

To create the evaluation set, the annotators were asked to first develop an understanding of the meaning of the Subject by inspecting up to 10 IC concepts which they were assigned to as individual tag (not by inheritance). After disambiguating the Subject label, the annotators looked up the matching candidates from AAT where they were told to primarily use the altLabels and the concepts hierarchy to disambiguate. When in doubt, they were instructed to further use the *Notes* which hold an explanation and in some cases a usage recommendation of the AAT concept. When both a broader and a narrower concept seemed fitting, both matches should be marked as correct.

Comparing the annotations of the two non-experts shows only a very low inter-rater agreement of 37%, which is an indicator of the difficulty of this task. Though the annotators marked about the same amount of connections as correct (45% and 49% of the matching candidates), their annotations still were very different.

For evaluating the performance of the matching system, both the intersection and the union of the connections marked as correct by the annotators were created, resulting in two ground truths, *union_truth* and *intersection_truth*, consisting of 90 and 138 correct links, respectively.

		Precision	Recall	F1
union	**this**	0.76	0.46	0.57
	all	0.57	1.00	0.73
intersection	**this**	0.59	0.54	0.57
	all	0.37	1.00	0.54

Table 1: Results of the presented algorithm (*this*) compared to an all-true baseline (*all*). As ground truth, *union_truth(union)* and *intersection_truth (intersection)* were used, respectively.

6.3. Results

The results of the matching evaluation can be found in Table 1. Precision, recall and F1 measure were calculated for both configurations, using *union_truth* and *intersection_truth* as ground truth. As all 1-to-0, 1-to-1 and 1-to-n matches must be taken into account, each connection was treated independently in the evaluation step. This means, that a matching candidate for the subject s_i which was discarded, though it was marked as correct in the ground truth, will be counted as a false negative, regardless of how other candidates for s_i were treated.

A baseline (*all*) was provided which does not consider disambiguation and marks all candidate matches as correct.

6.4. Discussion

The evaluation provided some fruitful insights on the difficulties of the task introduced. First, creating the evaluation set is a particularly challenging task, especially for non-experts. As there is no explicit definition, the meaning of IC Subjects has to be extracted via their assignment to different IC concepts. AAT concepts on the other hand tend to be very precise in meaning with only nuanced differences. In combination with the aforementioned varying specificity of IC Subjects, there is a lot of room for interpretation, which leads to the little agreement of the two annotators over the evaluation set.

The quantitative matching metrics in Table 1 show severe differences between the *union_truth* setting and the *intersection_truth* setting. Naturally, the precision of the baseline is higher in the *union_truth* setting, as more candidates are considered as correct. This together with the recall of 100% that arises with all-true classifiers creates a very high F1 score, which cannot be topped by the system presented in this paper, even though, its precision is at an acceptable level of 76%. For the *intersection_truth* setup, the presented algorithm can slightly beat the *all* baseline regarding the F1 measure, however both precision and recall are below 60%. This shows, that the cases that were more obvious to the human annotators not necessarily were as easy to distinguish for the system.

Taking a closer look at the produced matches on a qualitative level, different kinds off errors can be distinguished. A false positive match is categorised as "hard error" when the two entities that are aligned have completely different meaning, e.g., when the IC Subject *opening* which is for example assigned to the IC concept *31G332 opening of the book of life* is matched to the AAT *300002765 concept openings (architectural elements)* which describes *"apertures or breaks in the surface of a wall"*. "Soft errors" on the other side appear, when the (falsely) predicted matching entity is semantically close to the true entity or where the predicted matching entity and the true entity could be aggregated to a concept. For example, for the IC Subject *white poplar* (the tree) a proposed match to *white popular* (the wood) would be considered as soft error. Another example is the IC Subject *redingote* connected to the IC concept *41D211(REDINGOTE) dress, gown: redingote*, which is both matched with the AAT concept of the dress (300254632) and the concept of the overcoat (300209851). The evaluation against the *union_truth* resulted in 20 false-positive predictions, where only 8 were "hard error" and 12 were "soft errors".

When evaluating against the *union_truth*, 75 false-negative matches were produced , where over 70% (53) can be back-traced to 36 IC Subjects for which the algorithm did not predict any matches. For the vast majority of these IC Subjects, the created contexts did not overlap at all with the context of any of the matching candidates. This can either be an indicator for poor choice of context, or for the heterogeneity of the two resources resulting in completely different viewpoints and thus unmatchable contexts of the same concept.

7. Future Work

Many different approaches could be taken into account when trying to improve the interlinking of Iconclass Subjects and AAT concepts. First of all, the presented system could be adapted to achieve better results. For example, the defined context could be improved for both taxonomies. IC subjects' contexts could benefit from the removal of siblings and inherited siblings from Iconclass concepts from the main divisions 6 to 9, as these narrative Iconclass concepts add a lot of noise for the disambiguation algorithm. For AAT contexts, also *related* concepts could be added. Furthermore, the matching quality could benefit from adding post matching rules based on the resource knowledge, like Iconclass Subjects representing individuals or gods will not have a match in AAT, or IC Subjects describing trees should not match to wood concepts in AAT. Last but not least, a hyperparameter optimisation could be performed to find more suitable parameters than the experimental choice presented in this work. However, to find the most suitable and impactful actions, further analysis should be performed, starting by investigating the performance of the presented system on those IC Subjects with only one candidate match as well as the matching performance for other languages. Also, the evaluation process could be reconsidered, as false negatives could have too much weight in the current setting due to non-matching contexts. Another approach would be to rethink the matching strategy entirely, for example by adding external knowledge sources, which could potentially overcome the problem of low recall values.

Though IC Subjects exist in different languages, they are not interlinked. These can potentially be exploited in two of the following ways: Either, they can be taken into account during the disambiguation process, as ambiguities often do not persist across languages, or, the created matches can be used to interlink the IC Subjects, by leveraging the multilingual labels in AAT.

A platform and comprehensive interface for collaboratively suggesting, evaluating and correcting potential matches between Iconclass and AAT would offer great added value for the process of enriching Iconclass data. The availability of information that helps understanding the meaning of IC Subjects (e.g., IC concepts they are attached to) would accelerate this task. To facilitate the disambiguation of IC Subjects and to add another layer of semantic richness to Iconclass, IC Subjects could further be connected to a general purpose ontology, such as WordNet (Fellbaum, 1998).

Finally, the suitability for the matching algorithm proposed in this work for interlinking other resources could be explored. Though the approach was developed with the focus on disambiguating and interlinking tag-like objects associated with concepts in a source ontology with concepts of a target ontology, its generalistic definition makes it easily applicable to other data structures.

8. Conclusion

In this work, a matching and disambiguation algorithm to interlink IC Subjects with AAT concepts to improve semantic richness was introduced and its performance was investigated in a preliminary analysis. As ground truth served an evaluation set annotated non-expert. A quantitative analysis of the results shows rather moderate outcomes, though precision is always significantly above the baseline. This highlights the difficulty of the task (both for the algorithm and non-experts). A qualitative analysis provided important insights in remaining weaknesses of the system — especially in terms of recall — while showing that the system is able to produce promising predictions, as only a very limited number of false-positives are considered as "hard errors". Finally, several potential algorithmic improvements and research directions were suggested which are yet to be investigated.

9. References

David, R. and Kamerling, T. (2019). Relevancy Scoring for Knowledge-based Recommender Systems. In *IC3K 2019 - Proceedings of the 11th International Joint Conference on Knowledge Discovery, Knowledge Engineering and Knowledge Management*, volume 2, pages 233–239.

Fellbaum, C. (1998). *WordNet: An Electronic Lexical Database*. Bradford Book.

Peterson, T. (1990). Art & Architecture Thesaurus. *Oxford University Press*.

Van De Waal, H., Couprie, L. D., Tholen, E., and Vellekoop, G. (1973). *Iconclass : an iconographic classification system*. North-Holland Pub. Co., Amsterdam.

Weda, R. (2017). Bringing Two LOD Vocabularies Together. In *CIDOC Annual Conference*, pages 1–11, Tbilisi.

Proceedings of the 1st International Workshop on Artificial Intelligence for Historical Image Enrichment and Access (AI4HI-2020), pages 16–22
Language Resources and Evaluation Conference (LREC 2020), Marseille, 11–16 May 2020

Toward the Automatic Retrieval and Annotation of Outsider Art images: A Preliminary Statement

John Roberto, Diego Ortego[‡], Brian Davis
ADAPT Centre, [‡]INSIGHT Centre
Dublin City University, Glasnevin, Dublin 9, Ireland
{john.roberto, brian.davis}@adaptcentre.ie, diego.ortego@insight-centre.org

Abstract

The aim of this position paper is to establish an initial approach to the automatic classification of digital images about the Outsider Art style of painting. Specifically, we explore whether is it possible to classify non-traditional artistic styles by using the same features that are used for classifying traditional styles? Our research question is motivated by two facts. First, art historians state that non-traditional styles are influenced by factors "outside" of the world of art. Second, some studies have shown that several artistic styles confound certain classification techniques. Following current approaches to style prediction, this paper utilises Deep Learning methods to encode image features. Our preliminary experiments have provided motivation to think that, as is the case with traditional styles, Outsider Art can be computationally modelled with objective means by using training datasets and CNN models. Nevertheless, our results are not conclusive due to the lack of a large available dataset on Outsider Art. Therefore, at the end of the paper, we have mapped future lines of action, which include the compilation of a large dataset of Outsider Art images and the creation of an ontology of Outsider Art. This research forms part of a wider project called "Semantic Analysis of Text Corpora in the Outsider Art Domain".

Keywords: Outsider Art, visual aesthetics, artistic styles

1. Introduction

This paper is about the computational analysis of visual aesthetics. We focus our attention on Outsider Art, which is considered by some as the "unsightly style".

At present, aesthetics constitutes a field of interest for scientists working in Artificial Intelligence, particularly in the context of paintings. Five of the main tasks in this field are: the prediction of ratings, the detection of forgery in paintings, artist identification, genre recognition and style prediction. First, the prediction of ratings (Talebi and Milanfar, 2017) captures the technical and semantic level characteristics associated with emotions and beauty in images in order to categorize images in two classes: low and high quality. Second, the detection of forgery in paintings (Mane, 2017) assumes that an artist's brushwork is characterized by signature features that can be detected automatically. Third, "artist identification is the task of identifying the artist of a painting given no other information about it" (Viswanathan, 2017). Fourth, genre recognition in paintings (Agarwal et al., 2015) focuses on classifying works of art according to the (type of) scene that is depicted by the artist. Finally, style prediction uses both low-level and semantic features in order to group paintings according to their shared properties. Several studies on style prediction will be commented on this paper.

Recently, deep learning methods have been growing in popularity for style classification because they can achieve state-of-the-art performance in this field. For example, Deep Convolutional Neural Networks models such as AlexNet, VGGNet and ResNet have been applied to the classification of traditional painting styles with varying success thanks to the existence of large scale datasets of digital paintings. However, to the best of our knowledge, there are no attempts to classify, retrieve and annotate the Outsider Art style.

1.1. Traditional art styles

While the expression "artistic genre" is used to divide artworks according to the themes depicted (e.g. landscape, self-portrait, marine, religious, etc.), the term "artistic style" is used to refer to groups of works that have similar but not rigorously defined properties. This set of distinctive characteristics "permits the grouping of artworks into related art movements" (Bar et al., 2014). For example, Impressionism is characterised by the use of flurried brushstrokes to represent the subject with gesture and illusion (e.g. the painter Pierre-Auguste Renoir), Expressionism uses vivid and unrealistic colors to depict the subject as it appears to the artist (e.g. Wassily Kandinsky), in Abstraction the subject is reduced to its dominant colors, shapes or patterns (e.g. Piet Mondrian) and Baroque emphasize exaggerated motion and easily interpreted detail to produce drama and exuberance (e.g. Peter Paul Rubens). Figure 1 shows 5 different art styles, along with a brief description.

Art style divisions are often identified by art historians based on the experience of looking at other works of art and the historical context. However, this is not an easy task since the limits between art styles are vague or blurred. Indeed, a style can span many different painters, periods and artistic schools. For example, Goya's technique influenced both late Romanticism and Impressionism and Pablo Picasso painted in both surrealist and cubist styles.

1.2. Outsider Art and non-traditional art styles

Previous artistic styles are part of the mainstream art world, which means that they all have culture as "an inescapable aspect of image production" (Chadwick, 2015, p. 17). In practical terms, this means that a painter in the mainstream is inspired by the work of those who had gone before

Action Painting *paint is randomly splashed onto the canvas*

Contemporary Realism *depicts the real rather than the ideal*

New Realism *daily existence of common people*

Synthetic Cubism *simple geometric shapes, interlocking planes and collage*

Color Field Painting *large areas of a single colour*

Figure 1: Some examples of traditional artistic styles.

him/her but the artist is not conscious that he/she is "imitating" another work of art.

In contrast, there is the art created outside the boundaries of official culture or "Anti-cultural art" as described by Jean Dubuffet in 1949. The condition of "non-traditional" or, more specifically, "outsider" artist applies to people who have very little contact with the mainstream art world and for this reason have developed extreme unconventional ideas based on spontaneous inventions (see Figure 2a-b). We are therefore talking about psychiatric hospital patients, children, self-taught artists, people in prison or with autism, etc. The art of these "anti-intellectual, anti-professional, anti-academic" people (Cottom, 2003) resists analysis with traditional art criteria, while the use of non-artistic criteria such as personality features, prevents the consideration of the results of the creative process (you are looking at the person not at the work of art). This is the thinking of the Outsider art collector John Soldano, for whom "the only way for me to honestly define outsider art is by artists" and the arts writer Priscilla Frank who says that "while other genres like Abstract Expressionism or Cubism denote a specific set of aesthetic guidelines or artistic traditions, the label 'outsider art' reflects more the life story and mental or emotional aptitude of the artist" (Frank, 2017).

From a stylistic point of view, outsider artists paint obsessively repetitive images or themes (see Figure 2c). This might indicate an attempt to overcome the "horror vacui" (fear of empty space), bring order to mental chaos and provide reassurance that they are in control. It could be said that the outsider's vocabulary "oscillates back and forth between the ordered and monotonous filling of the surface of the work and the rhythmic and dynamic variation between the void and fullness of the composition" (Raw Vision magazine). Outsider Artists paint by physical impulse rather than intellectually. For that reason, subjects such as sexuality and eroticism can erupt in the most raw, emphatic and uncontrolled way (see Figure 2d). In some cases, the artworks appear to reveal dark desires which are not often played out in reality. These, and a number of other characteristics, make Outsider Art unattractive for a large part of the population and art historians.

In a larger sense, Outsider Art label covers an expanded range of non-traditional art styles such as art brut, naïve art, self-taught art, art singulier, visionary art, insane art, raw art, folk art, etc. All these form part of a continuum of artistic terms with blurred lines between them that are the tip of the iceberg of a potential task of classification of non-traditional art styles. In this article we use the terms **non-traditional** and **outsider** styles interchangeably.

(a) *Untitled* by Theodore H. Gordon (artbrut.ch)

(b) *Baby Beau Vine* by Lori Field (cumberlandgallery.com)

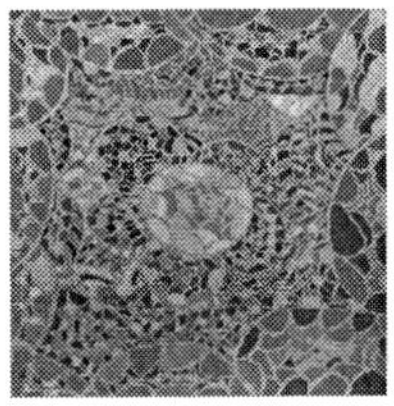

(c) *Untitled* (2016) by Stephanie Hill (creativegrowth.org)

(d) *Untitled* by Ramón Esteve (marginarte.com)

Figure 2: Some examples of Outsider Art paintings.

1.3. Classifying art style automatically in painting

Studies addressing the topic of the computational analysis of works of art are based on extracting a set of image features and using them to train different classifiers. Various formal image features such as line, color, texture or brush strokes and functional image features such as expression, content, composition and meaning (iconography) can be used to classify art styles automatically for paintings.

2. Related works

Classifying an artistic style automatically in painting has been the subject of much recent work that can be loosely divided into hand-crafted features and CNN-based features (training from scratch and pre-trained models). The former category (see Figure 3a) is a past tendency based in the use of computer vision methods to model handcrafted low-level features (e.g., color histograms, SIFT/GIST descriptor, texture, edges, brightness and gradient) that can be used by machine learning methods (e.g., SVM). The latter category (see Figure 3b) is a growing tendency and uses a Convolutional Neural Network (CNN) that encodes image content (semantic features) from a very large set of data (Zhao et al., 2017). Some examples of these two methods are briefly described below.

(a)

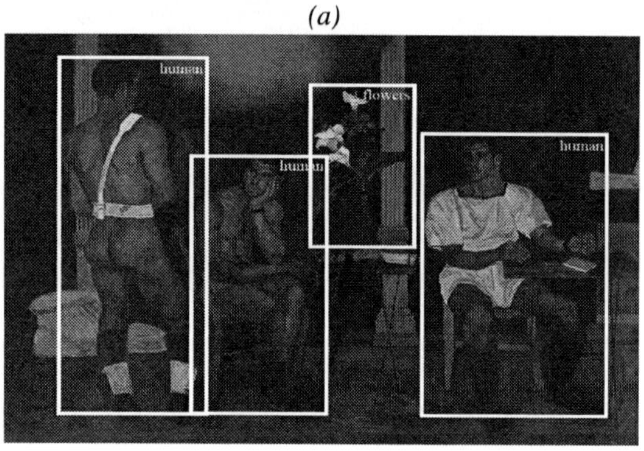

(b)

Figure 3: (a) low-level features (adapted from Condorovici et al. (2015) and (b) semantic features: object detection.

2.1. Handcrafted low-level features

Gunsel et al. (2005) trained an SVM classifier to discriminate between five painting styles. Their system computes a 6-dimensional vector of low level features. The authors report 90% accuracy with a low number of false positives. **Jiang et al. (2006)** classified traditional Chinese paintings into one of the two styles, Gongbi (traditional Chinese realistic painting) or Xieyi (freehand style) by using low-level features. They reported an accuracy rate of around 90% when combining decision tree and SVMs classifiers. **Wallraven et al. (2009)** tested how well several low-level features describe images from 11 different art periods. The authors found than "computational classifiers created from the participant data are able to categorize art periods with a performance of around 66%". The overall conclusion was that images grouped by humans corresponded better with the canonical art periods than those clustered by the computer.

Siddiquie et al. (2009) obtained good results in the classification of seven different painting styles by using multiple kernel learning in conjunction with low-level features (with accuracy rates of 76% to 92%). **Zujovic et al. (2009)** reported an overall accuracy rate of 69.1% when classifying five different genres. They used the AdaBoost classifier and, as features, steerable filters, as well as edge information extracted by a canny edge detector. **Shamir et al. (2010)** achieved an accuracy of 91.0% by using a set of low-level features on paintings by nine artists working in three different styles. **Culjak et al. (2011)** reported a 60.2% accuracy rate in the classification of six styles (including Naïve Art). They chose texture and color as low-level features and tested a range of classifiers, such as SVM.

Condorovici et al. (2015) achieved an overall detection rate of 72.24% on a database containing 4119 images from 8 painting styles (SVM). The authors selected features relevant for human perception and assessed the contribution of each feature. The overall conclusion is that the Dominant Color Volume features play a more important role for the automatic identification of artistic style.

2.2. CNN-based features

In the task of classifying 25 different painting styles from the Wikipainting dataset, **Karayev et al. (2014)** calculated through the confusion matrix up to 0.81 accuracy at predicting the Ukiyo-e style. They also found that the DeCAF, a deep CNN originally trained for object recognition, performs best for the task of classifying novel images according to their style. This leads them to conclude that some styles are closely related to image content, that is, the existence of certain objects in the painting.

Bar et al. (2014) examine binarized features derived from a Deep Neural Network in order to identify the style of paintings. They apply PiCoDes ("Picture Codes"), a very compact image descriptor, to learn a compact binary representation of an image. Their baseline was extracted from a CNN trained on the ImageNet dataset and implemented in Decaf, a deep convolutional activation feature for generic visual recognition. Their results show an improvement in performance with CNN-based features (0.43% accuracy) as well as their binarized version to distinguish 27 painting styles compared to hand-crafted low level descriptors (0.37% accuracy) such as Edge texture information and color histogram.

Mao et al. (2017) implemented DeepArt, a unified framework that can learn simultaneously both the contents and style of visual arts from a large number of digital artworks with multi-labels. The architecture of the framework is constructed by dual feature extraction paths that can extract style features and content features, respectively. The content feature representation path is generated on the basis of a VGG-16 network and the style feature representation path is built by adopting a Gram matrix to the filter responses in certain layers of the VGG-16 network. According to the authors, embedding the two output features in a single representation can be used to further improve two tasks: the automatic retrieval and annotation of digital artworks.

With the goal of outperforming the state-of-the-art, **Hong and Kim (2017)** trained a CNN on an art painting dataset of 30,000 distorted (projected, rotated, scaled, etc.) images to simulate real-world displaying conditions. Three different architectures of CNN were tested on this dataset: the first architecture was derived from AlexNet (Krizhevsky et al., 2012), the second architecture was inspired by VGGNet (Simonyan and Zisserman, 2014) and the third architecture was a smaller version of the second one which used a smaller filter size ($11 \rightarrow 7$) in the beginning and fewer neurons in fully-connected layers. The latter architecture performed best, obtaining low test error rates by optimizing its parameters with the Adam algorithm. According to the researchers, the proposed CNN-based method outperformed the previous state-of-the-art with a test error rate of 15.6% to 2%.

In order to identify the best training setup for the style classification of paintings, **Cetinic et al. (2018)** compared different CNN fine-tuning strategies performed on a WikiArt subset of 27 classes in which each class contains more than 800 paintings. They used visual features (e.g. edges or blobs) and content features (e.g. scenes and objects in paintings) derived from the layers of a CNN pre-trained on the ImageNet dataset (CaffeNet). Overall results indicate a lower accuracy for style classification due to the overlapping of visual properties between classes and the great diversity of content depicted in each style. The most distinctively categorized style was Ukiyo-e (84%) and the least distinctive was Academism, which was misclassified. On the basis of these results, researchers conclude that style is not only associated with mere visual characteristics and the content of paintings, but is often a contextually dependent concept.

Yang et al. (2018) argue that the style classification of painted images should consider the historical context in conjunction with traditional visual descriptors. Based on this observation, they built a multimodal CNN framework that considers origin time, birthplace and art movement in order to classify paintings into styles. Taking into account these three factors, Yang and colleagues achieved good performances on three datasets: 77.76% on Painting91 (13 style categories), 70.59% on OilPainting (17 image styles) and 73.28% on Pandora (12 art styles). They compared this multimodal method with single label method in the Painting91 dataset. The comparison results show that multimodal method can effectively identify painting style categories based on art history context knowledge.

Elgammal et al. (2018) adapted three main networks (AlexNet, VGGNet and ResNet) and variations in the training strategies for classifying 20 style classes. Their results showed that pre-training and fine-tuned networks outperform networks trained from scratch: with accuracy rates of 63.7% versus 55.2%. However, researchers consider that "the fine-tuned models could be outperformed if sufficient data is available to train a style-classification network from scratch". Additionally, by using Principle Component Analysis, they established that only few factors are discriminant enough to characterize different styles in art history. These factors are related to Wölfflin's five pairs modes of visual variation (Wölfflin, 1950): linear/painterly, planar/recessional, closed form/open form, multiplicity/unity, absolute clarity/relative clarity.

3. Preliminary experiments

Previous research has reported heterogeneous performances for the style classification of fine art paintings, depending on the type of features used and the number of categories created. Nevertheless, there is a significant degree of agreement on the prevalence of binarized features derived from a deep neural network over hand-crafted low level descriptors. But, can these findings be considered valid for non-traditional artistic styles? Such a question arises due to the fact that, as described in the Introduction, non-traditional styles are influenced by factors "outside" of the world of art. Additionally, Florea et al. (2016) showed that several artistic styles resist certain classification techniques.
Two different experiments were conducted in order to achieve a first approach to the classification of non-traditional styles. These experiments perform the binary and multiclass classification of Outsider Art and traditional styles.

3.1. Experimental setup

To study the performance correlation between Outsider Art and traditional styles, we trained, validated, and tested different networks using images from WikiArt and Outsider Art datasets. WikiArt is the largest public available dataset and contains 82,653 images classified in 27 artistic styles. It is fair to note that: *(i)* the "Wikiart collection [...] contains various paintings from different styles that are erroneously labeled" (Elgammal et al., 2018, p. 6) and *(ii)* this is an unbalanced dataset as seen in Figure 4. For its part, the Outsider Art dataset merges 2,405 images labeled as Naïve Art from WikiArt, which is considered very close to the Outsider Art style (Van Heddeghem, 2016, p. 13), and 1,232 Outsider Art images collected specifically for this paper (in total 3,616 images). In the experiments, the number of images and classes was reduced in order to work with balanced data.

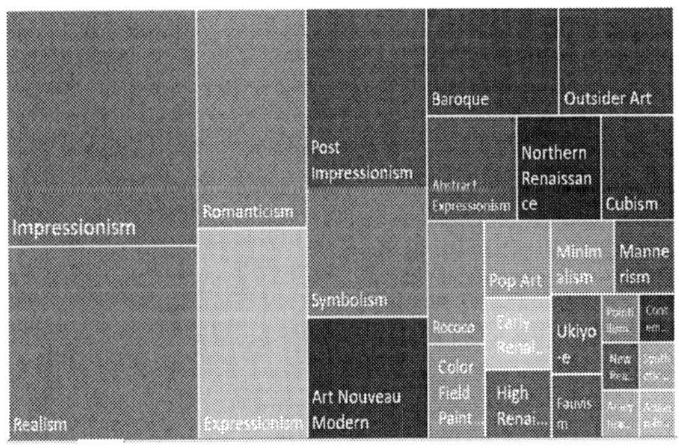

Figure 4: Original distribution of 27 styles: 26 traditional styles from WikiArt and the Outsider Art style (in the upper-right corner).

3.2. Classification from scratch

This experiment aims at answering the following scientific question: Does the Outsider style show a performance in the task of classifying paintings comparable to those of the

	Outsider	Cubism	Baroque	Abstract	Renaissance	Romanticism	Expressionism	Modern	Realism	Impressionism	%
Outsider	40,3	62,3	82,2	72,7	75	77,2	62,5	67,5	77	72	72,04
Cubism	62,3	40,9	82,5	77,1	68,9	76,5	58	66,5	76,4	70,6	70,98
Baroque	82,2	82,5	40,8	83,8	70	67,8	79,9	80	73,1	79,9	77,69
Abstract	72,7	77,1	83,8	44,3	79,2	80,2	73,5	70,1	81,1	80,6	77,59
Renaissance	75	68,9	70	79,2	37,2	71,9	67,7	70,3	73,9	75,3	72,47
Romanticism	77,2	76,5	67,8	80,2	71,9	42,5	70,9	70	62,3	71,3	72,01
Expressionism	62,5	58	79,9	73,5	67,7	70,9	40,1	62,3	71,9	66,2	68,10
Modern	67,5	66,5	80	70,1	70,3	70	62,3	42,5	72	67,5	69,58
Realism	77	76,4	73,1	81,1	73,9	62,3	71,9	72	37,5	64,3	72,44
Impressionism	72	70,6	79,9	80,6	75,3	71,3	66,2	67,5	64,3	46,9	71,97
	72,04	70,98	77,69	77,59	72,47	72,01	68,10	69,58	72,44	71,97	72,49

Figure 5: Accuracies between pairs of classes/styles.

traditional styles? To answer this question, we trained several Convolutional Neural Networks to classify different pairs of traditional and non-traditional artistic styles.

In this regard, WikiArt and Outsider Art datasets were used as basis categories for mapping the problem to multiple binary classification tasks (e.g. Cubism versus Outsider Art). Datasets were balanced by selecting 2,561 images per class and merging similar styles in ten basic categories: Cubism (CUB), Baroque (BAR), Abstract (ABS), Renaissance (REN), Romanticism (ROM), Expressionism (EXP), Modern Art (MOD), Realism (REA), Impressionism (IMP) and Outsider Art (OUT). As a result, the final dataset included 10 categories and **25,610** images that were resized to 28 × 21 pixels.

We trained several Convolutional Neural Networks from scratch using Keras API with Tensorflow as backend. Accuracies were obtained with 100 epochs because our tests indicate that using a number of epochs greater than 100 does not increase the performance significantly. Additionally, as is usually done in the literature, 70% of data were used for training, 20% of data for validation and 10% for testing. During the classification, all styles were crossed with each other in order to obtain the accuracies listed in Figure 5. The left hand column in the same Figure contains the average accuracy (%) obtained by each style.

In general, our results suggest that the task of classifying the Outsider Art style does not differ from classifying traditional styles. The classification of Outsider Art achieves a general average accuracy of 72,04%, which is below the average for Baroque (77,69%) and above the average for Expressionism (68,10%). This may indicate that, in contrast to what art historians state, this so-called anti-cultural art can be analyzed under the same parameters and conditions as mainstream art.

These preliminary results also show that Outsider Art is closely related to Cubism, Expressionism and Modern Art, resulting in poor accuracies (62.3%, 62.5% and 67.5%, respectively). Indeed, these three styles of art present the lowest average accuracy levels of the entire classification (70.9%, 69.5% and 68.1%, respectively). These analyses further show that while it is relatively easy for the classifier to differentiate Outsider Art from Baroque (82.2% of accuracy), Cubism and Expressionism are the pair of traditional styles that are more difficult to classify (58% of accuracy), while Baroque is the easiest style to classify.

However, although this seems obvious, it is important to emphasise that while style classification accuracies between pairs of styles are high (the estimated average efficiency levels are about 72,49%, see Figure 5), test accuracies drop dramatically when we classify three or more categories under a basic configuration: 3 styles/categories (62,4%), 4 styles/categories (52,2%), and so on, until the 10 styles (23,6%). In other words, it is essential to find features which can discriminate among multiple artistic styles. The second part of the following experiment tackles this issue.

3.3. Classification using a pre-trained model

This second experiment aims at answering the following scientific question: Is it possible to improve accuracy for Outsider Art style classification by using pre-trained models? Pre-trained models, such as ImageNet, VGGNet and ResNet use fine-tuned features that were originally trained on a different but correlated problem, to match the current problem. We trained a ResNet-18 model[1] to perform a **binary classification problem**: traditional versus Outsider Art styles. The dataset used is balanced, containing 2,028 images, 1,014 for Outsider Art and 1,014 for traditional art (homogeneously sampling 39 images for each of the 26 styles of traditional art from WikiArt). The test set is also balanced and has 416 images (208 for each category with the same sampling of 8 images for each of the 26 styles). The training is done for 40 epochs using pre-trained weights from ImageNet[2]. The batch size used is 128, weight decay 5e-4, momentum 0.9. Learning rate for blocks 1, 2 and 3 of ResNet-18 is set to 0.001 and the block 4 and the classifiers have a learning rate of 0.01. All learning rates are multiplied by 0.1 at epochs 20, 30 and 35. The model selected for classification is the one in the last epoch as no validation set was built due to the lack of data. The loss used is binary cross-entropy. Under this fine-tuned configuration, an accuracy of 84.3% was achieved. This accuracy outperforms all previous accuracies based on CNN trained from scratch, which means that repurposing and fine-tuning features can be used to obtain better feature rep-

[1]https://arxiv.org/abs/1512.03385

[2]https://ieeexplore.ieee.org/document/5206848

resentations of the Outsider Art style.
We have also trained a ResNet-18 model to perform a **multiclass classification problem**. The loss used is cross-entropy. The dataset is the same as that used in the experiment described in Section 3.2. with 224x224 crops extracted from the images resized to 256 in the smallest side (preserving the aspect ratio). The training was done for 120 epochs using pre-trained weights from ImageNet. Batch size used is 256, weight decay 5e-4, momentum 0.9. Initial learning rates are: for classifier 0.01, for blocks 3 and 4 0.001 and the rest of the parameters 0.0001. All learning rates are multiplied by 0.1 at epochs 70 and 100. The model selected for classification is the one in the best epoch of validation, whose accuracy is 61.17188 (see Figure 6). The test accuracy is 61.9141 (per class, Abstract: 0.9414, Baroque: 0.7891, Cubism: 0.8672, Expressionism: 0.5508, Impressionism: 0.5938, Modern: 0.5938, Outsider: 0.7695, Realism: 0.5273, Renaissance: 0.7695, Romanticism: 0.8047). This result agrees with the results from researchers in section 2.2., showing once again that there are no significant differences in classifying traditional and non-traditional art styles.

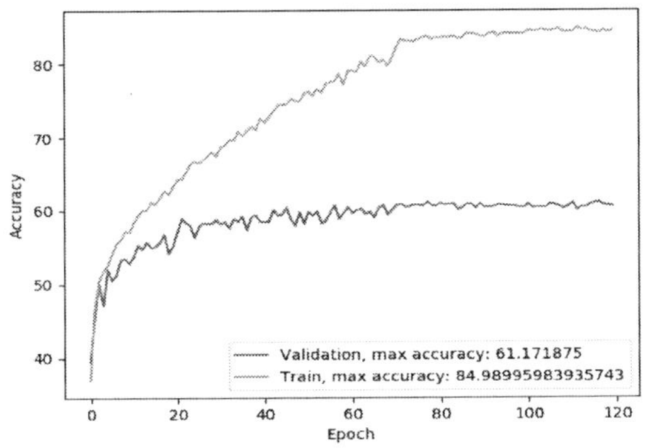

Figure 6: Validation and training accuracies with respect to the Epochs.

4. Conclusion and future work

This position paper has analysed the possibility of classifying non-traditional artistic styles by using the same binarized features that are used for classifying traditional styles. The first part of the paper introduces the theoretical elements that constitute a framework for understanding the problem. The second part describes the state-of-the-art on classifying art styles automatically in paintings. Due to the good accuracy performance of Deep Learning-based methods for classifying traditional art styles, it was suggested to apply them to classify non-traditional art styles (i.e. Outsider Art). Our preliminary experiments have provided good reasons to think that, as is the case with traditional styles, the Outsider Art can be computationally modelled by objective means.
Additionally, in accordance with theoretical (Frank, 2017) and applied (Yang et al., 2018) studies, we assume that the automatic classification of the Outsider Art style should consider **a multimodal approach based on an analysis of images, as well as text**. From our point of view, this two-fold strategy will involve (i) the compilation of a big dataset of Outsider Art images and (ii) the creation of an ontology of Outsider Art.
On the one hand, the image dataset will contain thousands of digital paintings in the Outsider Art style that can be used by machine learning algorithm. This resource can be integrated with the Outsider Art ontology to obtain a multimodal dataset for understanding Outsider Art, similar to that suggested by (Garcia and Vogiatzis, 2019).
On the other hand, the Outsider Art ontology will focus on representing part of our existing knowledge of this artistic style in a machine-readable language. A particular feature of the Outsider Art knowledge is that it includes both aesthetic entities and social/medical issues, for example: *"(Gaston Chaissac) suffered from tuberculosis, and for a time, produced art while convalescing in a sanitorium"* (Wikipedia). Therefore, the source text that we will use for ontology learning is a representative set of scientific books, papers, magazines and web pages. Additionally, we will integrate in our model some existing ontologies and terminologies such as the Conceptual Reference Model (CIDOC CRM) (Le Boeuf et al., 2019), the Europeana Data Model (EDM) (Europeana, 2017), the Art & Architecture Thesaurus (Alexiev et al., 2017)), the Cultural Objects Name Authority (CONA) (Harpring, 2019a), the Getty Iconography Authority (AI) (Harpring, 2019b) and the Getty Union List of Artist Names (ULAN) (Harpring, 2019c).
Currently, we are in the first phase of the project and aim to semi-automatically construct an exhaustive corpus that consists of semantically tagged texts. Our purpose is to apply this corpus to the construction of a large-scale corpus through the automatic retrieval and annotation of new texts. In the second phase of the project, we will extract the ontology from the corpus and we will use the ontology for automatic image annotation and retrieval.

5. Acknowledgements

This work has received funding from the Irish Research Council (Grant GOIPD/2019/463) and the ADAPT Centre for Digital Content Technology which is funded under the SFI Research Centres Programme (Grant 13/RC/2106). This research has been also supported by Science Foundation Ireland under grant number SFI/15/SIRG/3283.

6. Bibliographical References

Agarwal, S., Karnick, H., Pant, N., and Patel, U. (2015). Genre and style based painting classification. In *2015 IEEE Winter Conference on Applications of Computer Vision*, pages 588–594, Waikoloa Beach, Hawaii, January. IEEE.

Alexiev, V., Cobb, J., Garcia, G., and Harpring, P., (2017). *Getty Vocabularies: Linked Open Data version 3.4. Semantic Representation.* The Getty Vocabularies.

Bar, Y., Levy, N., and Wolf, L. (2014). Classification of artistic styles using binarized features derived from a deep neural network. *Computer Vision (Lecture Notes in Computer Science)*, 8925.

Cetinic, E., Lipic, T., and Grgic, S. (2018). Fine-tuning convolutional neural networks for fine art classification. *Expert Systems with Applications*, 114:107–118.

Chadwick, S. (2015). *Disorienting Forms: Jean Dubuffet, Portraiture, Ethnography*. Rice University, Houston, Texas.

Condorovici, R. G., Florea, C., and Vertan, C. (2015). Automatically classifying paintings with perceptual inspired descriptors. *Journal of Visual Communication and Image Representation*, 26:222–230.

Cottom, D. (2003). *Why Education Is Useless*. Phd. thesis, University of Pennsylvania Press.

Culjak, M., Mikuš, B., Jež, K., and Hadjic, S. (2011). Classification of art paintings by genre. In *Proceedings of the 34th International Convention*, pages 345—-369, Opatija: IEEE.

Elgammal, A., Mazzone, M., Liu, B., Kim, D., and Elhoseiny, M. (2018). The shape of art history in the eyes of the machine. In *32nd AAAI conference on Artificial Intelligence*, New Orleans, USA.

Europeana, (2017). *Definition of the Europeana Data Model v5.2.8*. European Union.

Florea, C., Condorovici, R., Vertan, C., Butnaru, R., Florea, L., and Vrăanceanu, R. (2016). Pandora: Description of a painting database for art movement recognition with baselines and perspectives. Proceedings of the European Signal Processing Conference (EUSIPCO).

Frank, P. (2017). What is the meaning of outsider art? the genre with a story, not a style.

Garcia, N. and Vogiatzis, G. (2019). How to read paintings: Semantic art understanding with multi-modal retrieval. In Stefan Roth et al., editors, *Computer Vision – ECCV 2018 Workshops, Proceedings*, volume 11130 of *Lecture Notes in Computer Science (including subseries Lecture Notes in Artificial Intelligence and Lecture Notes in Bioinformatics)*, pages 676–691, Germany, 1. Springer.

Gunsel, B., Sariel, S., and Icoglu, O. (2005). Content-based access to art paintings. volume 2, pages II – 558, 10.

Harpring, P., (2019a). *Cultural Objects Name Authority (CONA): Introduction and Overview*. Getty Vocabulary Program.

Harpring, P., (2019b). *The Getty Iconography Authority: Introduction and Overview*. Getty Vocabulary Program.

Harpring, P., (2019c). *The Getty Union List of Artist Names: Introduction and Overview*. Getty Vocabulary Program.

Hong, Y. and Kim, J. (2017). Art painting identification using convolutional neural network. *International Journal of Applied Engineering Research*, 12:532–539.

Jiang, S., Huang, Q., Ye, Q., and Gao, W. (2006). An effective method to detect and categorize digitized traditional chinese paintings. *Pattern Recognition Letters*, 27:734—-746.

Karayev, S., Hertzmann, A., Winnemoeller, H., Agarwala, A., and Darrell, T. (2014). Recognizing image style. In *Proceedings of the British Machine Vision Conference*, Nottingham, England. BMVA Press.

Krizhevsky, A., Sutskever, I., and Hinton, G. (2012). Imagenet classification with deep convolutional neural networks. *Advances in Neural Information Processing Systems*, 25:1106–1114.

Mane, S. (2017). Detection of forgery in art paintings using machine learning. *International Journal of Innovative Research in Science, Engineering and Technology*, 6:8681–8692.

Mao, H., Cheung, M., and She, J. (2017). Deepart: Learning joint representations of visual arts. In *Proceedings of the 25th ACM international conference on Multimedia*, Mountain View California, USA.

Shamir, L., Macura, T., Orlov, N., Eckley, D. M., and Goldberg, I. G. (2010). Impressionism, expressionism, surrealism: automated recognition of painters and schools of art. *ACM Transactions on Applied Perception (TAP)*, 7:1—-18.

Siddiquie, B., Vitaladevuni, S. N., and Davis, L. S. (2009). Combining multiple kernels for efficient image classification. In *Workshop on the Applications of Computer Vision (WACV)*, Snowbird, UT.

Simonyan, K. and Zisserman, A. (2014). Very deep convolutional networks for large-scale image recognition. In *3rd International Conference on Learning Representations (ICLR 2015)*, San Diego, CA.

Talebi, H. and Milanfar, P. (2017). *NIMA: Neural Image Assessment*. Institute of Electrical and Electronics Engineers (IEEE), San Diego, CA.

Van Heddeghem, R. (2016). *Outsider Art, In or Outside the World of Art? A study of the framing of the paradoxical position of outsider art*. Master thesis, Erasmus School of History, Culture and Communication, Erasmus University Rotterdam.

Viswanathan, N. (2017). Artist identification with convolutional neural networks. Technical report, Stanford University, California, USA.

Wallraven, C., Fleming, R., Cunningham, D., Rigau, J., F. M., and Sbert, M. (2009). Categorizing art: comparing humans and computers. *Computers and Graphics*, 33:484–495.

Yang, J., Chen, L., Zhang, L., Sun, X., She, D., Lu, S., and Cheng, M. (2018). Historical context-based style classification of painting images via label distribution learning. In *Proceedings of the 26th ACM international conference on Multimedia (MM '18)*, pages 1154–1162, New York, NY, USA.

Zhao, R., Wu, Z., Li, J., and Jiang, Y. (2017). Learning semantic feature map for visual content recognition. In *Proceedings of the 25th ACM international conference on Multimedia*, pages 1291–1299, New York, NY, USA. Association for Computing Machinery.

Zujovic, J., Gandy, L., Friedman, S., Pardo, B., and Pappas, T. N. (2009). Classifying paintings by artistic genre: an analysis of features and classifiers. In *International Workshop on Multimedia Signal Processing*, Rio De Janeiro: IEEE.

Proceedings of the 1st International Workshop on Artificial Intelligence for Historical Image Enrichment and Access (AI4HI-2020), pages 23–28
Language Resources and Evaluation Conference (LREC 2020), Marseille, 11–16 May 2020

Automatic Matching of Paintings and Descriptions in Art-Historic Archives using Multimodal Analysis

Christian Bartz*, Nitisha Jain*, Ralf Krestel
Hasso Plattner Institute
University of Potsdam, 14482 Potsdam, Germany
{firstname.lastname}@hpi.de

Abstract

Cultural heritage data plays a pivotal role in the understanding of human history and culture. A wealth of information is buried in art-historic archives which can be extracted via digitization and analysis. This information can facilitate search and browsing, help art historians to track the provenance of artworks and enable wider semantic text exploration for digital cultural resources. However, this information is contained in images of artworks, as well as textual descriptions or annotations accompanied with the images. During the digitization of such resources, the valuable associations between the images and texts are frequently lost. In this project description, we propose an approach to retrieve the associations between images and texts for artworks from art-historic archives. To this end, we use machine learning to generate text descriptions for the extracted images on the one hand, and to detect descriptive phrases and titles of images from the text on the other hand. Finally, we use embeddings to align both, the descriptions and the images.
Keywords: cultural heritage, keyphrase identification, machine learning, natural language processing, computer vision

1. Introduction

In the age of big data, there is increasing attention on the digitization of cultural heritage collections and their availability as digital libraries to aid wider access and exploration of this previously opaque data. A number of museums, libraries, and other cultural institutions (e.g. Europeana, Getty Research Institute, Wildenstein Plattner Institute, and the Rijks Museum[1]) have invested significant efforts to digitize their collections consisting of old art books, catalogues for art exhibitions and auctions, etc. Initiatives, such as OpenGLAM[2], promote collaboration among these cultural institutions for research on shared resources.

The volume and heterogeneity of these digitized collections necessitates automated analysis of this data. Modern data science tools can assist in deriving insights from the images, as well as from the textual content of these collections. In addition to the actual content, cultural heritage datasets, such as art-historic corpora, are often enriched with meta-data that can provide useful information and context for automatic tools. One example of meta-data is the associations between the artwork images and the texts contained in catalogues and books. Art-historic corpora contain textual information in the form of captions of images (often depicting the titles of artworks), as well as the description of artworks including their creator, year, and, in case of auction catalogues, price information. During the digitization step, images from physical pages are typically scanned and the text is retrieved by means of Optical Character Recognition (OCR) technology. Although these techniques have been fairly improved to minimize the error rate, the information about the association between the images of artworks and their corresponding text excerpts is not retained. This is especially true when multiple images and text excerpts are present on a single page. The availability of such associations between images and texts can help with multimodal semantic analysis of artworks, wherein important descriptive features can be identified from the images, while the corresponding text might provide additional background information about the style and context of the artwork and the artist. In some cases, the text can also provide further evidence and confirmation for the features inferred from the images, and vice versa. For example, consider a case where image analysis correctly ascertains that a particular painting depicts a house with mountains in the background, and the associated text description not only contains terms such as mountains and house but also mentions that this painting is in landscape orientation, then the painting can be categorized and tagged as such. This meta-data derived from the associations between images and texts could be particularly useful in search and exploration of lost artworks, where only a few indicators about the sought-out artworks are known beforehand. An art historian would greatly benefit from image-text associations while retrieving images of artworks from a database by searching on the basis of a few keywords (style, motif, orientation and other features) that can be found in the corresponding description texts.

The matching of images with texts can be done at various levels of granularity based on the size of the data under consideration. Each level poses different challenges and demands unique techniques to achieve desired results. For instance, multiple images on a single catalogue page have a higher likelihood to belong to a common theme or topic. Matching at this level requires techniques to differentiate between similar images, as well as to extract the most distinctive keyphrases from the text descriptions. When the task is scaled to a large corpus of multiple types of catalogue pages, the matching will need to be performed between a large number of possible pairs. To narrow down the search space, the images could be classified on the basis of their art styles by identifying and leveraging common themes in the corpus. This would be followed by matching

*both authors contributed equally

[1] www.europeana.eu, www.getty.edu/research, wpi.art, www.rijksmuseum.nl

[2] openglam.org

on basis of differentiating characteristics as before.

In this work, we propose a generic framework to retrieve the associations between images of artworks and texts from art-historic archives by means of automated approaches. Due to the multimodal nature of this task, our solution is comprised of a combination of techniques from computer vision, as well as natural language processing. While image captioning techniques are employed to identify and tag the images of artworks, Named Entity Recognition (NER) and keyphrase identification techniques are used for the extraction of descriptive terms from the text excerpts. Lastly, to establish the associations between the images and texts, we perform the representation and alignment of the description texts obtained from above techniques via embeddings.

This paper describes an ongoing project on multimodal analysis of cultural heritage datasets. The project is a part of a larger collaboration[3] with the Wildenstein Plattner Institute[4] that was founded to promote scholarly research on cultural heritage collections. The contributions of this paper are : (1) Introduce the novel task of matching artwork images to their text descriptions in art-historic corpora. (2) Propose a framework to extract descriptive features from images and texts of artworks and perform their semantic alignment. (3) Identify evaluation methods for measuring the performance of the framework.

2. Related Work

The multimodal nature of our proposed framework is rooted in two different fields. The first field is text analytics for automatic understanding of the semantics of extracted texts. The second field is image analysis for the extraction of the semantics of images. In this section, we present and outline the relation of previous work that is related to the analysis of cultural heritage data for each of the two fields.

2.1. Text Analytics

Analysis of cultural heritage data has been of active research interest for the digital humanities where various works have performed use case driven text analysis of digitized art corpora. For example, there is existing work on performing event extraction for historical events (Segers et al., 2011) and finding parallel passages from cultural heritage archives (Harris et al., 2018). There have been several attempts to create knowledge repositories in the form of knowledge graphs and linked open data collections from art data (Hyvönen and Rantala, 2019; Van Hooland and Verborgh, 2014; Dijkshoorn et al., 2018; De Boer et al., 2012). While these works lay emphasis on extracting facts and useful information from the text, they do not necessarily identify the most representative terms and keyphrases from the text. NER is a related task which has been performed for the cultural heritage domain in several papers (Van Hooland et al., 2013; Ehrmann et al., 2016; Jain and Krestel, 2019). The challenges of this task in the context of noisy OCRed datasets have been discussed previously (Rodriquez et al., 2012) and (Kettunen and Ruokolainen, 2017). While we also require techniques to handle noise in datasets as proposed by these papers, this is not the primary focus of our work. For our text analytics approach, we need to broaden the scope beyond NER to identify the most important phrases from the digitized texts that contain descriptions of the artworks, which has not been addressed by any previous work.

2.2. Image Analysis

Automatic image analysis in the domain of art-historical research has been studied in several earlier research works (Huang et al., 2018; Elgammal et al., 2018; Yang et al., 2018; Thomas and Kovashka, 2019). One of the greatest problems of automatic image analysis in the art domain is the availability of suitable training data (Huang et al., 2018; Elgammal et al., 2018; Thomas and Kovashka, 2019). Methods in related work rely on fine-tuning image classification models, pre-trained on photographs, to overcome the problem of the non-availability of training data. Using such pre-trained models often leads to the problem of domain-adaptation, which arises because available models are pre-trained on photos and not on images of artworks. Thomas and Kovashka (Thomas and Kovashka, 2019) propose to use methods of neural style transfer (Gatys et al., 2015) to generate a sufficient amount of training data, based on photographs and a set of artworks that are used as baseline style images. All in all, related methods mainly concentrate on the problem of image classification (Thomas and Kovashka, 2019), style, genre, and artist classification (Huang et al., 2018; Elgammal et al., 2018; Lecoutre et al., 2017), or time period and type classification (Yang et al., 2018). So far, there has been no work on performing automatic image captioning for artworks, which is one of the focus points of our work.

2.3. Combination of Text Analysis and Image Analysis

A natural idea is to embed the features extracted from both modalities into a common semantic subspace (Kiros et al., 2014; Liu et al., 2019), where a model is learned, that embeds text and image features in a shared high dimensional embedding space. The goal of the embedding is to bring the concepts, obtained from text and image analysis that have the same meaning, as close to each other as possible. In our work, we want to follow this basic embedding approach and use the combined information from text analysis models and image analysis models for the matching of an image to its corresponding text in art-historic corpora.

3. Matching Paintings and Descriptions

In this section, we discuss our proposed framework for performing the matching of artwork images to associated texts and describe the different components in detail. We envision to create an automated pipeline that takes the raw scan of a page of any catalogue or book as input and performs several operations on it: (1) Text is localized and recognized using off-the-shelf OCR software. (2) The text analysis component extracts the most representative terms with help of NER and keyphrase identification. (3) In parallel, images on each page are localized and the image analysis

[3] `https://hpi.de/naumann/projects/web-science/caart.html`

[4] `https://wpi.art/`

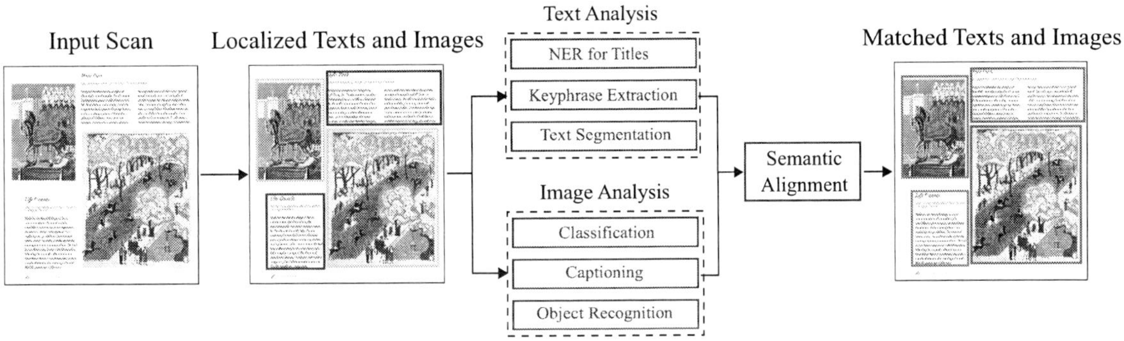

Figure 1: Overview of proposed framework

component extracts semantic meta-data from each image. (4) In the semantic alignment component, the results of step (1) and step (2) are embedded into a shared space and are used for matching and linking of the images to texts. Figure 1 provides a structural overview of the proposed framework. In the remainder of this section, we will explain the challenges and possible approaches towards a solution for each of the sub-tasks, namely text analysis, image analysis and semantic alignment of text and images.

3.1. Text Analysis

An intuitive way to match an image in an art catalogue with its description is via the *title* of the artwork. Assuming that the description of any given artwork will include the title, a human would be able to identify the relevant image on the page by matching the title with the caption of the image. Since any caption text associated with the images (including their titles) is usually not available after the digitization process, the matching for digitized datasets has to be performed solely on the basis of the features or tags that are extracted from the images. However, matching on the basis of titles alone is still not a viable approach due to several reasons. Firstly, as discussed in (Jain and Krestel, 2019), the identification of titles of artworks in textual descriptions is itself a non-trivial task and shows sub-optimal performance with existing NER tools. Secondly, even for a scenario where the titles are correctly identified from the text descriptions, they are not always sufficiently representative of the artworks. An example would be modern art paintings where the titles may not be descriptive of the motif in the painting and thus not helpful for matching. Titles are also not useful in the case of old portrait paintings where it is difficult to uniquely identify an image from the name of the depicted person (which is also the title in most cases). This illustrates that titles of artworks might not necessarily contain the required semantic information for the matching of texts with artwork images. As our approach relies on semantic alignment for the matching, it is important to focus on identifying the most salient parts of the description of paintings in the text.

To this end, there are two methods we would like to investigate. The first is to look at *keyphrase extraction*, which identifies and extracts the most representative phrases from a document. Supervised approaches for keyphrase identification are popular (Jiang et al., 2009), however they need annotated training data which is tricky to generate for art datasets. Owing to the subjective nature of the domain, a gold standard training dataset is difficult to obtain due to lack of agreement by non-expert annotators. Therefore, in this work, we would like to turn to unsupervised keyphrase extraction techniques (Hasan and Ng, 2010; Mihalcea and Tarau, 2004) where the task is performed with help of semantic relatedness. Further, to fine-tune this task for the art domain, we want to pursue domain-specific keyphrase extraction techniques (Wu et al., 2005; Hulth et al., 2001).

The second method is to directly *embed the text* in the semantic space. For this approach, we would need to perform the segmentation of the text excerpts, followed by identification of the relevant segments that contain descriptions of the artwork images. This is important particularly for art books where the texts include discussions not only about artworks, but also about the artists, art styles, etc.

3.2. Image Analysis

In order to analyze the semantic content of digitized images, we plan to use modern computer vision methods based on deep learning. Computer vision tasks which are very close to the tasks that we want to perform, are automatic image classification (Krizhevsky et al., 2012), image captioning (Xu et al., 2015), i.e. the generation of textual desciptions of depicted content, and object detection (Ren et al., 2015). All of these methods extract semantic information from images and have been shown to work very well on photographs. The most challenging problem in working with images of artworks is that photographs have a very different underlying data distribution than images of artworks, especially paintings. This makes it necessary to train machine learning models directly on images of artworks. However, large-scale annotated training data sets with artworks are not available.

There exist some datasets that contain artworks and annotations (e.g. art style), such as the WiKiArt database[5], or the OmniArt dataset (Strezoski and Worring, 2018). However, none of these datasets can be used for image classification or automatic image captioning, since they lack the annotations required for these tasks. We can, however, make use of photographies and their annotations, which are available in large-scale datasets.

[5] https://www.wikiart.org

To this end, we want to follow (Thomas and Kovashka, 2019) and use methods of neural style transfer (Gatys et al., 2015; Yao et al., 2019) to create new large-scale art centered datasets for image classification, image captioning, and object recognition on artworks. For image classification, we want to use the ImageNet dataset (Deng et al., 2009) and create a new ArtImageNet dataset that we will use as a base model in a subsequent step to train an image classification model. For image captioning and object detection, we want to use the COCO dataset (Lin et al., 2014) and fine-tune the image classification model that we created earlier for each of these tasks. For creating the artistic versions of the photographs from each dataset, we want use the WikiArt or the OmniArt dataset, as artistic style images.

3.3. Semantic Alignment

After performing the extraction of meaningful features from textual data and image data in parallel, the next step is to find ways of aligning the extracted information and match an image to its accompanying text. For this, we want to embed the output from the text analysis and image analysis component in a common semantic space (i.e via word embeddings), where we can represent similar concepts close to each other and thereby find text and image pairs that might be a good match. Another idea, is to use the feature vectors created by the image analysis methods and train a further model to embed them into the same semantic space as the word embeddings of the relevant texts and phrases. Such an alignment in a common semantic subspace will allow us to perform image retrieval for a given text query and also text retrieval for a given query image.

4. Evaluation Methods

In this section, we address the question of the evaluation of the proposed framework. This question can be divided into three parts: 1) How to evaluate the proposed text analysis methods regarding their adjustments to fit the challenges of extracting relevant information from art-historic archives. 2) How to evaluate the proposed image analysis methods in the context of art analysis, since state-of-the-art image analysis methods are mainly trained on photographs, which are quite different from artworks. 3) How to evaluate the framework that performs the alignment of the information from the text and image analysis components to enable matching of images with their textual descriptions.

Evaluation of Text Analysis. As discussed in Section 3.1., the availability of annotated datasets for training and evaluation is a major bottleneck for evaluating semantic representations, especially in the art domain. For this, we plan to enlist the help of domain experts for the creation of a smaller gold standard test dataset that will include annotations for the most important textual segments or keyphrases for identifying the corresponding images. The performance of our text analytics approaches can then be measured by comparing the results with the gold standard annotations in terms of precision and recall.

Evaluation of Image Analysis. The most important aspect in evaluating the image analysis methods is how well they can be adapted to work on images of art, despite having only a very small amount of annotated real training data available. Though there are datasets available, e.g. provided by Europeana[6], their annotations do not follow a common scheme which limits their utility for our purpose. As we propose in Section 3.2., we want to use methods of neural style transfer to create a sufficient amount of training data. On the one hand, we want to focus on the plain numerical evaluation of these models, using well known evaluation metrics, like classification accuracy for image classification, precision, recall and f-measure, as well as average precision for object detection, and metrics for image captioning evaluation, e.g. BLEU-score (Papineni et al., 2002), METEOR (Banerjee and Lavie, 2005), CIDEr (Vedantam et al., 2015), ROUGE (Lin, 2004), SPICE (Anderson et al., 2016), BERTScore (Zhang et al., 2019), or MoverScore (Zhao et al., 2019). On the other hand, we are interested in evaluating the influence of different base models that are used to create our image captioning for art, or object detection models. Here, we want to compare a standard ImageNet model with a model created with our ArtImageNet dataset. We want to use this to examine whether automatic methods can successfully be used to generate novel annotated data, based on already available data.

Evaluation of Text and Image Alignment. The task of matching a given text to an image in an art catalogue can be cast as a retrieval task. This retrieval task consists of two aspects. The first aspect is to retrieve an image, given a textual description and the second is to retrieve a textual description, given an input image. We can use standard image retrieval evaluation methods, also used in related work (Kiros et al., 2014; Liu et al., 2019), such as recall at k ($R@K$), for the evaluation. Here, we are interested in different values of K based on the granularity of the current search. If we only consider a single page with text and several images, we are interested in the recall at $K = 1$, whereas if we want to retrieve an image to a given text over an entire catalogue, we are interested in the performance at higher values of K. Since the problem of extracting images and their textual descriptions from art-historic archives has not been studied before, there are no evaluation datasets available. For the evaluation of our method, it will be important to create an evaluation dataset with help from domain experts that includes different levels of granularity, for measuring the performance of this kind of retrieval task.

5. Conclusion

In this paper, we present the description of a project that deals with the novel task of matching artwork images to their corresponding text descriptions in digitized art-historic corpora. We provide an overview of the related work and challenges in this domain and describe a possible framework to tackle the problem of image and text alignment. Furthermore, we give an overview of the possible evaluation methods that we want to use for evaluating each component as well as the overall performance of our proposed framework.

Acknowledgement. We thank the Wildenstein Plattner Institute for providing access to their art-historic archives.

[6]https://www.europeana.eu/en/collections/topic/190-art

6. References

Anderson, P., Fernando, B., Johnson, M., and Gould, S. (2016). SPICE: Semantic Propositional Image Caption Evaluation. In *Proceedings of the European Conference on Computer Vision*, pages 382–398.

Banerjee, S. and Lavie, A. (2005). METEOR: An automatic metric for MT evaluation with improved correlation with human judgments. In *Proceedings of the ACL Workshop on Intrinsic and Extrinsic Evaluation Measures for Machine Translation and/or Summarization*, pages 65–72.

De Boer, V., Wielemaker, J., Van Gent, J., Hildebrand, M., Isaac, A., Van Ossenbruggen, J., and Schreiber, G. (2012). Supporting Linked Data Production for Cultural Heritage Institutes: The Amsterdam Museum Case Study. In *Proceedings of the Extended Semantic Web Conference*, pages 733–747.

Deng, J., Dong, W., Socher, R., Li, L., Li, K., and Fei-Fei, L. (2009). ImageNet: A large-scale hierarchical image database. In *Proceedings of the IEEE Conference on Computer Vision and Pattern Recognition*, pages 248–255.

Dijkshoorn, C., Jongma, L., Aroyo, L., Van Ossenbruggen, J., Schreiber, G., ter Weele, W., and Wielemaker, J. (2018). The Rijksmuseum Collection as Linked Data. *Semantic Web*, 9(2):221–230.

Ehrmann, M., Colavizza, G., Rochat, Y., and Kaplan, F. (2016). Diachronic Evaluation of NER Systems on Old Newspapers. In *Proceedings of the 13th Conference on Natural Language Processing (KONVENS)*, pages 97–107.

Elgammal, A., Liu, B., Kim, D., Elhoseiny, M., and Mazzone, M. (2018). The Shape of Art History in the Eyes of the Machine. In *Proceedings of the Thirty-Second AAAI Conference on Artificial Intelligence*.

Gatys, L. A., Ecker, A. S., and Bethge, M. (2015). A Neural Algorithm of Artistic Style. *arXiv:1508.06576 [cs, q-bio]*.

Harris, M., Levene, M., Zhang, D., and Levene, D. (2018). Finding Parallel Passages in Cultural Heritage Archives. *Journal on Computing and Cultural Heritage*, 11(3):1–24.

Hasan, K. S. and Ng, V. (2010). Conundrums in Unsupervised Keyphrase Extraction: Making Sense of the State-of-the-art. In *Proceedings of the 23rd International Conference on Computational Linguistics*, pages 365–373.

Huang, X., Zhong, S.-h., and Xiao, Z. (2018). Fine-Art Painting Classification via Two-Channel Deep Residual Network. In *Advances in Multimedia Information Processing – PCM 2017*, pages 79–88.

Hulth, A., Karlgren, J., Jonsson, A., Boström, H., and Asker, L. (2001). Automatic Keyword Extraction using Domain Knowledge. In *Proceedings of the International Conference on Intelligent Text Processing and Computational Linguistics*, pages 472–482.

Hyvönen, E. and Rantala, H. (2019). Knowledge-based Relation Discovery in Cultural Heritage Knowledge Graphs. In *Digital Humanities in the Nordic Countries*, pages 230–239.

Jain, N. and Krestel, R. (2019). Who is Mona L.? Identifying Mentions of Artworks in Historical Archives. In *Proceedings of the International Conference on Theory and Practice of Digital Libraries*, pages 115–122.

Jiang, X., Hu, Y., and Li, H. (2009). A Ranking Approach to Keyphrase Extraction. In *Proceedings of the 32nd International ACM SIGIR Conference on Research and Development in Information Retrieval*, pages 756–757.

Kettunen, K. and Ruokolainen, T. (2017). Names, Right or Wrong: Named Entities in an OCRed Historical Finnish Newspaper Collection. In *Proceedings of the 2nd International Conference on Digital Access to Textual Cultural Heritage*, pages 181–186.

Kiros, R., Salakhutdinov, R., and Zemel, R. S. (2014). Unifying Visual-Semantic Embeddings with Multimodal Neural Language Models. *arXiv:1411.2539 [cs]*.

Krizhevsky, A., Sutskever, I., and Hinton, G. E. (2012). ImageNet Classification with Deep Convolutional Neural Networks. In *Advances in Neural Information Processing Systems 25*, pages 1097–1105.

Lecoutre, A., Negrevergne, B., and Yger, F. (2017). Recognizing Art Style Automatically in Painting with Deep Learning. In *Proceedings of the Asian Conference on Machine Learning*, pages 327–342.

Lin, T.-Y., Maire, M., Belongie, S., Hays, J., Perona, P., Ramanan, D., Dollár, P., and Zitnick, C. L. (2014). Microsoft COCO: Common Objects in Context. In *Proceedings of the European Conference on Computer Vision*, pages 740–755.

Lin, C.-Y. (2004). ROUGE: A package for automatic evaluation of summaries. In *Proceedings of Workshop on Text Summarization Branches out, Post2Conference Workshop of ACL*.

Liu, Y., Guo, Y., Liu, L., Bakker, E. M., and Lew, M. S. (2019). CycleMatch: A cycle-consistent embedding network for image-text matching. *Pattern Recognition*, 93:365–379.

Mihalcea, R. and Tarau, P. (2004). TextRank: Bringing Order into Text. In *Proceedings of the Conference on Empirical Methods in Natural Language Processing*, pages 404–411.

Papineni, K., Roukos, S., Ward, T., and Zhu, W.-J. (2002). BLEU: A Method for Automatic Evaluation of Machine Translation. In *Proceedings of the 40th Annual Meeting on Association for Computational Linguistics*, pages 311–318.

Ren, S., He, K., Girshick, R., and Sun, J. (2015). Faster R-CNN: Towards Real-Time Object Detection with Region Proposal Networks. In *Advances in Neural Information Processing Systems 28*, pages 91–99.

Rodriquez, K. J., Bryant, M., Blanke, T., and Luszczynska, M. (2012). Comparison of Named Entity Recognition Tools for Raw OCR Text. In *Konvens*, pages 410–414.

Segers, R., Van Erp, M., Van Der Meij, L., Aroyo, L., van Ossenbruggen, J., Schreiber, G., Wielinga, B., Oomen, J., and Jacobs, G. (2011). Hacking History via Event Extraction. In *Proceedings of the 6th International Conference on Knowledge Capture*, pages 161–162.

Strezoski, G. and Worring, M. (2018). OmniArt: A Large-scale Artistic Benchmark. *ACM Transactions on Multimedia Computing, Communications, and Applications*, 14(4):88:1–88:21.

Thomas, C. and Kovashka, A. (2019). Artistic Object Recognition by Unsupervised Style Adaptation. In *Proceedings of the Asian Conference on Computer Vision ACCV 2018*, pages 460–476.

Van Hooland, S. and Verborgh, R. (2014). *Linked Data for Libraries, Archives and Museums: How to Clean, Link and Publish your Metadata*.

Van Hooland, S., De Wilde, M., Verborgh, R., Steiner, T., and Van de Walle, R. (2013). Exploring Entity Recognition and Disambiguation for Cultural Heritage Collections. *Digital Scholarship in the Humanities*, 30(2):262–279.

Vedantam, R., Lawrence Zitnick, C., and Parikh, D. (2015). CIDEr: Consensus-Based Image Description Evaluation. In *Proceedings of the IEEE Conference on Computer Vision and Pattern Recognition*, pages 4566–4575.

Wu, Y.-f. B., Li, Q., Bot, R. S., and Chen, X. (2005). Domain-Specific Keyphrase Extraction. In *Proceedings of the 14th ACM International Conference on Information and Knowledge Management*, pages 283–284.

Xu, K., Ba, J., Kiros, R., Cho, K., Courville, A. C., Salakhutdinov, R., Zemel, R. S., and Bengio, Y. (2015). Show, Attend and Tell: Neural Image Caption Generation with Visual Attention. In *Proceedings of the 32nd International Conference on Machine Learning, ICML 2015*, pages 2048–2057.

Yang, S., Oh, B. M., Merchant, D., Howe, B., and West, J. (2018). Classifying Digitized Art Type and Time Period. In *Proceedings of the 1st Workshop on Data Science for Digital Art History-Tacking Big Data*.

Yao, Y., Ren, J., Xie, X., Liu, W., Liu, Y.-J., and Wang, J. (2019). Attention-Aware Multi-Stroke Style Transfer. In *Proceedings of the IEEE Conference on Computer Vision and Pattern Recognition*, pages 1467–1475.

Zhang, T., Kishore, V., Wu, F., Weinberger, K. Q., and Artzi, Y. (2019). BERTScore: Evaluating Text Generation with BERT. *arXiv:1904.09675 [cs]*.

Zhao, W., Peyrard, M., Liu, F., Gao, Y., Meyer, C. M., and Eger, S. (2019). MoverScore: Text Generation Evaluating with Contextualized Embeddings and Earth Mover Distance. In *Proceedings of the 2019 Conference on Empirical Methods in Natural Language Processing and the 9th International Joint Conference on Natural Language Processing(EMNLP-IJCNLP)*, pages 563–578.

Proceedings of the 1st International Workshop on Artificial Intelligence for Historical Image Enrichment and Access (AI4HI-2020), pages 29–33
Language Resources and Evaluation Conference (LREC 2020), Marseille, 11–16 May 2020

Towards a Comprehensive Assessment of the Quality and Richness of the Europeana Metadata of Food-related Images

Yalemisew Abgaz, Amelie Dorn, Gerda Koch, Jose Luis Preza Diaz
Adapt Centre Dublin City University, Austrian Academy of Sciences, European-Local Austria
Dublin Ireland, Vienna Austria, Graz Austria
Yalemisew.abgaz@adaptcentre.ie, kochg@europeana-local.at
{Amelie.Dorn,JoseLuis.PrezaDiaz }@oeaw.ac.at,

Abstract

Semantic enrichment of historical images to build interactive AI systems for the Digital Humanities domain has recently gained significant attention. However, before implementing any semantic enrichment tool for building AI systems, it is also crucial to analyse the quality and richness of the existing datasets and understand the areas where semantic enrichment is most required. Here, we propose an approach to conducting a preliminary analysis of selected historical images from the Europeana platform using existing linked data quality assessment tools. The analysis targets food images by collecting metadata provided from curators such as Galleries, Libraries, Archives and Museums (GLAMs) and cultural aggregators such as Europeana. We identified metrics to evaluate the quality of the metadata associated with food-related images which are harvested from the Europeana platform. In this paper, we present the food-image dataset, the associated metadata and our proposed method for the assessment. The results of our assessment will be used to guide the current effort to semantically enrich the images and build high-quality metadata using Computer Vision.

Cultural image analysis, Semantic enrichment, Computer Vision, Ontology, Knowledge design

1. Introduction

As a result of open access policy (European Commission, 2011) adopted by Galleries, Libraries, Archives and Museums (GLAMs), a huge collection of cultural and historical resources is now available on the internet to promote access. Many GLAMs started to publish digital resources and the associated metadata to support ease of search and retrieval by both humans and computer agents (Abgaz et al., 2018; Stork et al., 2019). However, a significant portion of the resources still lacks quality and rich metadata. In some cases, the available metadata only describes basic bibliographic information such as title and the publication year of the resource. Often, the interpretation and utilisation of the data by users other than subject experts are hampered by the lack of domain knowledge and machine-readable rich semantics to understand the dataset.

By rich semantics, we mean that the availability of multiple descriptors of a resource including bibliographic information, domain-specific annotation, links to interconnected resources, etc. By quality, we refer to a multitude of metrics including the correctness, reuse of existing terms, use of multiple languages, etc. defined in (Zaveri et al., 2015; Debattista et al., 2016; Debattista et al., 2018). The availability of rich semantics enables the exploitation of the metadata in several creative ways by both humans and machines, whereas ensuring the quality enables to build dependable systems which produce high-quality results.

There have been efforts made to provide joint platforms and standard tools to aggregate and publish data from GLAMs. Europeana.eu [1] is one of such platforms established by the European Union as a virtual aggregator of digitised collections from more than 3,500 institutions across Europe. This platform brings together contributing institutions and Europeana local platforms to aggregate content, facilitate knowledge transfer and innovation, distribute cultural heritage content and engage users to participate in the use and contribution of the resources via a centralised platform supporting multilingual and multi-faceted search and retrieval of the available resources (Haslhofer and Isaac, 2011; Isaac and Haslhofer, 2013). Cultural and historical collections including images, pictures, paintings, photographs, specimen, etc. are at the primary focus of Europeana. The Europeana effort started in 2008 and the current collection still suffers from a lack of rich metadata for many of its objects. As these metadata emerge from many different contributors, there are still many discrepancies (both in coverage and semantics) in the richness and quality of the metadata despite the effort made to standardise using the European Data Model (EDM) [2] (Haslhofer and Isaac, 2011).

In this position paper, we present our proposed approach for analysing the quality and semantic richness of selected images related to food by taking the Europeana collection as a cases study. Even if there is a consensus on the importance of analysing the quality and richness of the whole Europeana collection, in this paper, we will focus on analysing the coverage and the quality of the semantic annotation of food-related images using food-related domain-specific ontologies and thesauri. By historical images, we refer to the collection of images, pictures, paintings and photographs that represent some historical or cultural importance. It is observed that even if the collection is enriched with metadata of some kind, the historical, cultural and domain-specific aspects of the data are underrepresented by the available metadata. The metadata is not semantically enriched to reflect the detailed content of the images. This problem is partially demonstrated during the evaluation of the quality of search results obtained from the platform when users search the collection using historical and cultural aspects. It further requires a meticulous investiga-

[1] https://www.europeana.eu/portal/en

[2] https://pro.europeana.eu/resources/standardization-tools/edm-documentation

tion to identify the strength and weaknesses of the metadata in representing the detailed aspects of the cultural images. In this research paper, we present our research questions followed by our proposed approach. The questions are:

- How much semantic annotation is available for food-related images and what is the quality of the available metadata?
- How rich is the domain-specific annotation in using multiple vocabularies?
- What aspects (technical, social, cultural, political, etc.) of the images are semantically well annotated?
- What are the gaps that are observed in the metadata and how can we address it using semantic enrichment?

Our focus is on historical images related to food. So far we collected 65 buckets of food images representing particular food topics. These images are used to analyse the semantic richness and quality of the metadata in depth. The Europeana images contain associated metadata which can be downloaded through a special functionality provided to us by the Europeana Local-Austria. We have collected all the metadata (semantic annotations) of the images in JSON and RDF formats. We will use this metadata throughout to evaluate the quality and richness of the metadata.
This paper is organised in five sections. Section 2. introduces Europeana and the coverage of the collection followed by some discussion of relevant research in Section 3. Section 4. presents the data collection process, the target food image collection and the metadata. Section 5. presents the proposed approach and metrics to be used and, finally, we present the conclusion and future work in Section 6.

2. Background

Europeana is an aggregator platform which provides central access to resources from GLAMS. The platform allows users to search all the collections that are distributed across several institutions in Europe from a single search interface. However, Europeana does not host the original digital objects on its servers but provides metadata about the items and dereferenceable links to the institutions that hold the collections. This approach allows Europeana to maintain the level of aggregation required to support search and retrieval of information, and it enables the institution to keep and continuously improve the collection and the associated metadata while the original data stays in the content providers' websites. Europeana uses metadata from the providers and maps this metadata using EDM (Isaac, 2013; Innocenti, 2014) to provide a single common interface for efficient and searchable information.
Currently, Europeana offers access to about 60 million items including books, music, artworks and more[3]. But Europeana's aim is not only to aggregate the metadata but also to involve content providers in the very challenging task of improving the quality of the metadata by achieving good quality metadata for 70% of their collections. This is achieved through the use of enrichment tools to improve the existing metadata and by assisting content providers to follow new quality frameworks.

3. Related Research

Previous research has been conducted to determine the quality of the Europeana metadata. Peter et al. Király et al. (2019; Kirly and Bchler (2018) evaluated the data quality in Europeana focusing on its multilinguality. The authors defined metrics for evaluating the multilinguality using metrics such as completeness, consistency, conformity and accessibility. Even if this paper provides good coverage of the metrics used in determining multilinguality, its focus is only on a language-related quality measure. In our proposed method, we would like to widen the scope and include other quality metrics available elsewhere and also measure the diversity of the metadata concerning the coverage of the subject matter presented in the image collection.
Other metrics proposed in (Gavrilis et al., 2015) present a quality measure in metadata repositories. The authors proposed five metrics together with some contextual parameters concerning metadata generation and use. The quality measures the authors use include completeness, accuracy, appropriateness, consistency and auditability. These metrics also overlap with the metrics used to evaluate the multilinguality of the metadata. However, they incorporate contextual parameters such as a requirement for higher accuracy using weightings of the metrics. They evaluated their metrics using Europeana data of the archaeology aggregator CARARE (Connecting ARchaeology and ARchitecture for Europeana).
Generic and comprehensive data quality measures are also proposed by (Debattista et al., 2016) incorporating 24 metrics distributed across four major categories. These metrics also measure the quality of metadata and present the results using percentages. The approach also provides a customisable implementation of the metrics which can be used based on the specific requirements of the evaluation. We will initially consider all the metrics that are covered in the paper and later filter those that are not applicable. A followup paper (Debattista et al., 2018) has also used a Europeana dataset to demonstrate the applicability of the proposed metrics, however, the detail of the analysis reported in the paper is not sufficient to make any concrete decision regarding the quality of the metadata. Thus, it is important to use the proposed metrics to drill down and investigate the selected quality issues.

4. Data Collection

For this study, we use digital images and their associated metadata collected from the Europeana online image collection. In the whole repository, there are more than 58 million digital objects (images, texts, audios, videos and 3D objects) available with the associated metadata describing mainly the bibliographic information of the objects.

4.1. Food Images

For this study, we restrict our focus on digital images including paintings, photos, drawings and sketches. Since conducting a deep analysis on the full collection is beyond the scope of our project, we narrow down the focus only

[3]https://www.europeana.eu/portal/en/about.html

Search Topic	Items	Topic	Items	Search Topic	Items
Alimentation sistemas culinarios	838	Food and Nederland s	122	Lebensmittel+	1773
Breakfast	100	Food and Norway	280	Lunch	363
Cafe	123	Food and party	29	Painting and Food	182
Comedor	36	Food and people	465	Painting and Fruit	484
Dessert	532	Food and Portugal	60	Panaderia	307
Drawings and Illustrations	98	Food and shop	1968	Photograph and Breakfast	45
Eating	880	Food and shopping	152	Photograph and Dinner	28
Food and autumn	11	Food and society	366	Photograph and Eating	20
Food and Belgium	127	Food and Spain	48	Photograph and Food	63
Food and celebration	64	Food and sports	12	Photograph and Fruit	207
Food and cuisine	27	Food and spring	55	Photograph and Lunch	41
Food and culture	9445	Food and summer	25	Print and Food	5
Food and customs	16	Food and Sweden	758	Produccion y alimentos	4060
Food and dancing	27	Food and Switzerland	52	Reposteria	394
Food and Denmark	32	Food and traditions	47	Soup	300
Food and family	216	Food and winter	37	Speisesaal	244
Food and Finland	100	Food and woman	64	Still life	354
Food and France	227	Food and work	130	Still life and Food	8765
Food and Germany	180	Food+Austria	4986	Lebensmittel	627
Food and Luxembourg	33	Food+machine	396	Godigital	6
Food and man	280	Frhstck	38	Gastronomy	1100
Food and market	119				
Total					**42969**

Table 1: The distribution of the images across different buckets

to food-related images. This is due to the following reasons. First, food is associated with our daily life and it is one of the most familiar topics for humans to deal with. Second, food represents the culture and the history of both traditional and modern society. We also have food-related images that cover a long period from the early centuries to the modern-day. Third, food is highly interconnected to several other disciplines including health, fitness, nutrition, economics, business, culture, society, agriculture, technology, politics, etc. This allows us to analyse the richness of the metadata associated with food and to evaluate the coverage of these aspects of food in the available metadata. Finally, since this analysis is being conducted in the context of the ChIA[4] project (accessing and analysing cultural images with new technologies), the focus is on testing the quality of the existing semantic enrichment of cultural food images to improve access and enhance analysis using artificial intelligence applications such as chatbots to support interactive search. Results from this project will not only enable wider access possibilities for Europeana images but also provide increased semantic capabilities for Digital Humanity researchers to work with image-related data.
So far we have collected images from the Europcana plat form including photos, paintings, drawings using 64 non-exclusive buckets. These images are collected by using several food-related keywords prepared by experts from socio-linguistic, computer science, and digital humanity domains. A total of 42,969 images are collected and included in the analysis. Table 1 summarises the distribution of food images across the search topics.

4.2. Metadata

We use a platform provided by the Europeana Local-Austria team to download both the images and the metadata. For all the selected images, the metadata is available in a JSON and RDF format which is provided in the EDM standard. Depending on the provider, additional metadata is also available for most of the images. This indicates that

[4]https://chia.acdh.oeaw.ac.at/

Figure 1: Sample image with its metadata.

there is some uniformity in the usage of bibliographic data across all the images, however, the use of additional metadata fields and ontologies largely depends on the provider of the image. A sample image is shown in Figure 1 and a snippet of the associated metadata is given the text below.


```
{
"object": {
"about": "/2059513/data_foodanddrink_efd_LGMA_0933",
"aggregations": [
  {
   "about": "/aggregation/provider/2059513/
          data_foodanddrink_efd_LGMA_0933",
      "edmDataProvider": {
       "def": [
            "Local Government Management Agency"]},
      "edmIsShownBy": "http://griffiths.askaboutireland.ie/gv4/dev/
             fandd_images/selection_of_breads_and_butter.jpg",
      "edmObject": "http://griffiths.askaboutireland.ie/gv4/dev/
             fandd_images_thumbs/selection_of_breads_and_butter.jpg",
      "edmProvider": {
            "def": [
            "Europeana Food and Drink"] },
      "edmRights": {
      "def": [    "http://creativecommons.org/licenses/by-sa/3.0/"]},
                  ...
      "concepts": [
      {
            "about": "http://data.europeana.eu/concept/base/48",
            "prefLabel": {
                  "de": ["Bild (Fotografie)"],
                  "fi": ["Valokuva"],
                  "ko": ["  "],
      ...
```


Since all the metadata related to an image is downloaded into a single file, the number of metadata files in the collection is equal to the size of the images. The metadata in RDF can be directly used by the selected quality assessment tool. This metadata will be analysed for its quality using specific metrics and following a sampling approach, we also consider a manual evaluation of the descriptive nature of the associated metadata compared to the actual image. Even if this task consumes a significant amount of time, it is worth to check the quality going a little beyond what the automated analysis tools provide. This metadata is further used to analyze the richness of the metadata in describing the concepts/aspects depicted in the image. This looks into potential ontologies, vocabularies and thesauri in the food domain and checks how many of them are used across the images to semantically annotate the images.

5. Proposed Assessment Approach

We considered two types of quality measures applicable to the assessment of the quality and richness of the metadata. The first is using quantitative measures where objective metrics are used to analyze quality based on some mathematical formula, and the second one is a qualitative approach where an expert judgement is required to determine the quality. In this work, we will use both methods in such a way that existing widely used objective metrics are selected and used to evaluate the quality and the richness of all the metadata of the selected images. The qualitative evaluation focuses on a deep analysis of the metadata by comparing it with the corresponding image and evaluate how much of the explicit and implicit information contained in the target image is represented by the metadata. In this particular approach, we will use experts from the food domain to qualitatively evaluate the selected images and the corresponding metadata to evaluate both the quality and the richness of the metadata. This approach complements the quantitative approach with expert judgement on the accuracy and correctness of the metadata and identifies the gap between the potentially useful information contained in the image and what is represented in the metadata.

5.1. Quality Analysis Tools and Metrics

Several researchers have identified and proposed metadata quality metrics including the 67 metrics and 18 quality dimensions (Zaveri et al., 2015) and 27 metrics implemented (Debattista et al., 2016). The later metrics are also implemented in a linked data quality assessment framework (Luzzu). Due to its comprehensive and deployable tool, we conduct an initial experiment with the Luzzu framework to quantitatively analyze the quality of our dataset. The metrics included in the Luzzu framework are categorised into four major categories (Debattista et al., 2016): representational, where the focus is on the design of the data in terms of common best practices and guidelines; contextual category, which focuses on the relevance, correctness, understandability and timeliness; intrinsic category, which focuses on correctness and coherence of the data including syntactic validity, semantic accuracy, consistency, conciseness and completeness; and accessibility category, which focuses on the (re)usability of linked data resources by both machines and humans. All these categories contain relevant metrics for our dataset. However, not all the metrics are directly useful for the work we are conducting, such as the length of the characters in a URI. Thus, we carefully select the metrics we use to assess the quality of the metadata

5.2. Semantic Richness Analysis

Zavier et al Zaveri et al. (2015) further identified metrics that are used to determine the richness of the metadata: detection of good quality interlinks, the existence of links to external data providers and dereferenced back-links. However, in (Debattista et al., 2016) interlinking is included in the accessibility metrics. In analysing the richness of the metadata, even if these metrics measure how richly the metadata is connected with other sources, our main interest is to check whether these external links are connected to domain-specific ontologies, vocabularies, thesauri which give detailed context and meaning to the contents of the images. This requires a further analysis of the external links included in the metadata and evaluating whether these links point to domain-specific or bibliographic metadata.
To achieve this objective, we identify major domain-specific ontologies (Dooley et al., 2018), vocabularies[5] (Harpring, 2018; Caracciolo et al., 2013; Leatherdale et al., 1982) and thesauri in the areas of the topics of the selected datasets. Mainly, we narrowed down our focus to food-related metadata to evaluate the semantic richness in providing useful information for supporting educators, scientists and even content providers to focus more on the semantic enrichment using domain-specific metadata which makes the collection more relevant to the users.

6. Conclusion

In this paper, we present the current work we are conducting to evaluate the quality and the richness of the metadata of a selected set of food image collections from Europeana to identify gaps of the current semantic enrichment. To this end, we selected 42,969 images and the associated metadata for the evaluation. We proposed both qualitative and quantitative evaluation methods with existing scientifically proven methods and metrics. So far, we have identified most of the relevant metrics, selected the framework and acquired the relevant data. Our next step will be to apply the method and evaluate the quality and richness of the dataset using the proposed methods. One of the challenging tasks is the qualitative evaluation of the richness and the contextual accuracy of the metadata compared to the contents of the images. To address this issue, we will incorporate evaluators from the three categories of Europeana users: the educators, scientists, and content providers to evaluate the richness and the correctness of the metadata.

Acknowledgements:
This research is funded by the Austrian Academy of Sciences under the funding scheme: go!digital Next Generation (GDNG 2018-051). The ChIA project is carried out in collaboration with the ADAPT SFI Research Centre at Dublin City University. The ADAPT SFI Centre for Digital Media Technology is funded by Science Foundation Ireland through the SFI Research Centres Programme and is co-funded under the European Regional Development Fund (ERDF) through Grant # 13/RC/2106.

[5]http://www.getty.edu/research/tools/vocabularies/aat/help.html

7. Bibliographical References

Abgaz, Y., Dorn, A., Piringer, B., Wandl-Vogt, E., and Way, A. (2018). Semantic modelling and publishing of traditional data collection questionnaires and answers. *Information*, 9(12).

Caracciolo, C., Stellato, A., Morshed, A., Johannsen, G., Rajbhandari, S., Jaques, Y., and Keizer, J. (2013). The agrovoc linked dataset. *Semant. Web*, 4(3):341348, July.

Debattista, J., Auer, S., and Lange, C. (2016). Luzzua methodology and framework for linked data quality assessment. *J. Data and Information Quality*, 8(1), October.

Debattista, J., Lange, C., Auer, S., and Cortis, D. (2018). Evaluating the quality of the lod cloud: An empirical investigation. *Semantic Web*, 9(1):131–150.

Dooley, D. M., Griffiths, E. J., Gosal, G. S., Buttigieg, P. L., Hoehndorf, R., Lange, M. C., Schriml, L. M., Brinkman, F. S. L., and Hsiao, W. W. L. (2018). Foodon: a harmonized food ontology to increase global food traceability, quality control and data integration. *npj Science of Food*, 2(23).

European Commission. (2011). Commission recommendation of 27 october 2011 on the digitisation and online accessibility of cultural material and digital preservation. Technical report, European Commission.

Gavrilis, D., Makri, D.-N., Papachristopoulos, L., Angelis, S., Kravvaritis, K., Papatheodorou, C., and Constantopoulos, P. (2015). Measuring quality in metadata repositories. In Sarantos Kapidakis, et al., editors, *Research and Advanced Technology for Digital Libraries*, pages 56–67, Cham. Springer International Publishing.

Harpring, P. (2018). Getty vocabularies: Linked open data version 3.4. semantic representation.

Haslhofer, B. and Isaac, A. (2011). data.europeana.eu: The europeana linked open data pilot. *International Conference on Dublin Core and Metadata Applications*, 0:94–104.

Innocenti, P. (2014). *Migrating Heritage: Experiences of Cultural Networks and Cultural Dialogue in Europe*. Ashgate.

Isaac, A. and Haslhofer, B. (2013). Europeana linked open data - data.europeana.eu. *Semantic Web*, 4:291–297, 01.

Isaac, A. (2013). Europeana data model primer. Technical report, European Commission.

Király, P., Stiller, J., Charles, V., Bailer, W., and Freire, N. (2019). Evaluating data quality in europeana: Metrics for multilinguality. In Emmanouel Garoufallou, et al., editors, *Metadata and Semantic Research*, pages 199–211, Cham. Springer International Publishing.

Kirly, P. and Bchler, M. (2018). Measuring completeness as metadata quality metric in europeana. In *2018 IEEE International Conference on Big Data (Big Data)*, pages 2711–2720.

Leatherdale, D., Tidbury, G. E., Mack, R., Food, of the United Nations., A. O., and of the European Communities., C. (1982). *AGROVOC : a multilingual thesaurus of agricultural terminology / Donald Leatherdale ; with the collaboration of G. Eric Tidbury and Roy Mack*. Apimondia, by arrangement with the Commission of the European Communities [S.l.], english version. edition.

Stork, L., Weber, A., Miracle], E. G., Verbeek, F., Plaat, A., [van den Herik], J., and Wolstencroft, K. (2019). Semantic annotation of natural history collections. *Journal of Web Semantics*, 59:100462.

Zaveri, A., Rula, A., Maurino, A., Pietrobon, R., Lehmann, J., and Auer, S. (2015). Quality assessment for Linked Data: A survey. *Semantic Web Journal*.

Association for Computational Linguistics
209 N. Eighth Street
Stroudsburg, Pennsylvania 18360

ISBN 978-1-7138-1253-1

9 781713 812531

CURRAN ASSOCIATES INC.
proceedings.com